Dramatic Story Structure

A successful screenplay starts with an understanding of the fundamentals of dramatic story structure. In this practical introduction, Edward J. Fink condenses centuries of writing about dramatic theory into ten concise and readable chapters, providing the tools for building an engaging narrative and turning it into an agent-ready script. Fink devotes chapters to expanding on the six basic elements of drama from Aristotle's *Poetics* (plot, character, theme, dialogue, sound, and spectacle), the theory and structure of comedy, as well as the concepts of unity, metaphor, style, universality, and catharsis. Key terms and discussion questions encourage readers to think through the components of compelling stories and put them into practice, and script formatting guidelines ensure your finished product looks polished and professional. *Dramatic Story Structure* is an essential resource not only for aspiring screenwriters, but also for experienced practitioners in need of a refresher on the building blocks of storytelling.

Edward J. Fink, Ph.D., is Professor and Chair of Radio-TV-Film at California State University, Fullerton.

Dramatic Story Structure

A PRIMER FOR SCREENWRITERS

edward j. fink

NEW YORK AND LONDON

First published 2014
by Routledge
711 Third Avenue, New York, NY 10017

Simultaneously published in the UK
by Routledge
2 Park Square, Milton Park, Abingdon, Oxon OX14 4RN

Routledge is an imprint of the Taylor & Francis Group, an informa business

© 2014 Taylor & Francis

The right of Edward J. Fink to be identified as author of this work has been asserted by him in accordance with sections 77 and 78 of the Copyright, Designs and Patents Act 1988.

All rights reserved. No part of this book may be reprinted or reproduced or utilised in any form or by any electronic, mechanical, or other means, now known or hereafter invented, including photocopying and recording, or in any information storage or retrieval system, without permission in writing from the publishers.

Trademark notice: Product or corporate names may be trademarks or registered trademarks, and are used only for identification and explanation without intent to infringe.

Library of Congress Cataloging-in-Publication Data
Fink, Edward J.
 Dramatic story structure : a primer for screenwriters / Edward J. Fink.
     pages cm
  Includes bibliographical references and index.
  1. Motion picture authorship. 2. Television authorship. I. Title.
 PN1996.F454   2013
 808.2'3—dc23
 2013007413

ISBN: 978-0-415-81369-3 (hbk)
ISBN: 978-0-415-81371-6 (pbk)
ISBN: 978-0-203-06798-7 (ebk)

Typeset in Bembo
by Apex CoVantage, LLC

Printed and bound by CPI Group (UK) Ltd, Croydon, CR0 4YY

To my wife Friederike and my children Anna and Liam, who keep the good drama in my life.

Contents

Preface	xiii
Acknowledgments	xv
1. Introduction and Sample Script	1
Drama Defined	1
Aristotle and Others	2
Sample Script: *La Llorona (The Weeping Woman)*	4
2. Plot	11
Three-Act Structure	11
Act 1: Setup to New Direction	16
Act 2A: Launch of Journey to Midpoint Crisis	19
Act 2B: All Goes Well to All is Lost	23
Act 3: Turnaround to Climax and Denouement	26
Throughout all Three Acts	29
Experiments with Three-Act Structure	31
Sample Plot Points	33
Jule Selbo's 11 Steps (2007)	34
Chris Vogler's 12 Steps (2007), based on Campbell (1949)	35

Eric Edson's 23 Steps (2011)	37
Summary	40
Reflection and Discussion	42

3. Character   44

Protagonists	44
Extraordinary Person in Ordinary Situation	47
Ordinary Person in Extraordinary Situation	47
Achilles' Heel	48
Arc	49
Antagonists	51
Human v. Human	52
Human v. Environment	53
Human v. Self	54
Supporting Characters	55
Functionaries	57
Unmasking	58
Ethos, Pathos, and Hybris	59
Experiments with Character	62
Character Types	63
Four Humors	64
Enneagram	65
Sigmund Freud (1856–1939)	66
Carl Jung (1875–1961)	66
Myers-Briggs	67
Lajos Egri (1888–1967)	68
Obsession	69
Summary	71
Reflection and Discussion	72

4. Theme — **73**

- What Theme Is Not: Plot or Character — **73**
- What Theme Is: Lesson with Point of View — **74**
- Typologies of Theme — **76**
- Treatment of Theme — **77**
- Experiments with Theme — **79**
- Summary — **81**
- Reflection and Discussion — **82**

5. Dialogue — **84**

- Show, Don't Tell — **84**
- Creating Dialogue — **86**
  - *Poeticism* — **86**
  - *Naturalism* — **88**
  - *Realism* — **89**
  - *Heightened Realism* — **91**
- Functions of Dialogue — **93**
  - *Advance Plot* — **93**
  - *Reveal Character* — **93**
  - *Point to Theme* — **94**
- Comprehensibility — **96**
- Memorable Lines — **99**
- Dual Meaning — **102**
- Summary — **103**
- Reflection and Discussion — **103**

6. Sound — **106**

- Sound for Screenwriters — **106**
- Music — **107**

Diegetic, Nondiegetic, and Metadiegetic	**108**
Parallel and Counterpoint	**109**
Sound Effects	**111**
Voice	**112**
Summary	**114**
Reflection and Discussion	**115**
7. Spectacle	**116**
Spectacle for Screenwriters	**116**
Locations and Sets	**118**
Location or Studio	**119**
Interior or Exterior	**120**
Physical or Virtual	**120**
Realistic or Nonrealistic	**120**
Lights and Shadow	**121**
Costume and Wardrobe	**123**
Hair and Makeup	**125**
Properties	**127**
Actors' Physical Features	**127**
Blocking and Camera Shots	**128**
Special Effects	**130**
Editing	**131**
Summary	**133**
Reflection and Discussion	**133**
8. Unity, Metaphor, Universality, Catharsis, and Style	**135**
Unity	**135**
Unity of Action	**135**
Unity of Time and Place	**136**
Unity of Theme	**137**

Contents   xi

Metaphor	**139**
Universality	**141**
Catharsis	**142**
Style	**144**
Realism and Nonrealism	**144**
Tragedy and Comedy	**146**
Summary	**149**
Reflection and Discussion	**149**

9. Comedy   **151**

High and Low Comedy	**151**
Schadenfreude and *Mudita*	**156**
Three Grand Theories of Comedy: Incongruity, Superiority, and Psychoanalytic (Relief)	**158**
Incongruity Theory	**158**
Superiority Theory	**162**
Psychoanalytic or Relief Theory	**164**
Comic Structure	**166**
Setup and Payoff	**166**
Rule of Threes	**167**
Running Gag	**168**
Double Whammy	**168**
Innuendo and Double Entendre	**169**
One-Liners and Put-Downs	**170**
Summary	**171**
Reflection and Discussion	**172**

10. Script Formats   **174**

Screenplay Format	**176**
Sitcom Format	**182**

Contents

Two-Column, Split-Page, AV Format	**183**
Stage-Play Format	**190**
Summary	**194**
Reflection and Discussion	**195**
References	**197**
Index	**205**

Preface

The objective of this book is to condense centuries of writing about dramatic theory into a concise and readable manuscript on the fundamental principles of dramatic story structure. Entire libraries explore in great depth the many facets of the world of drama. As an introductory primer, this book is not intended to exhaust all these theories and techniques, but to draw from their commonalities, distilling the most basic concepts into around 200 pages (55,000 words). As such, this text targets those who are beginning to study screenwriting, either in a classroom or on their own, and would like an introductory book that lays out the basics before moving to more advanced tomes by any of the many screenwriting gurus. This manuscript also targets more experienced writers who would like a refresher of the fundamentals of story. Writing instructors, too, will find this book useful, and they can bring their own perspectives and additional materials to supplement this text in their classes.

The structure of this book is straightforward. The first chapter provides an introductory overview and a sample short script that serves as a common example throughout the text. Chapters 2–7 examine the six elements of drama discussed by Aristotle in *The Poetics* (c. 335 BCE), the first widely-regarded theoretical discussion of drama: plot, character, theme, dialogue, music (sound), and spectacle. An eighth chapter discusses five additional concepts: unity, metaphor, style, universality, and catharsis. The dramatic form of tragedy is implied and covered in these chapters, so Chapter 9 offers an additional discussion of comedy, specifically comic theory and structure. Chapter 10 is applied, presenting a primer in the formats for four different kinds of plays: screenplay, sitcom, two-column, and stage play.

Throughout this text, **bold type** denotes a term in the index and *italic type* denotes emphasis or a foreign word or title.

Acknowledgments

I wish to thank so many people who helped make this text a reality: Routledge Publishing Company, especially Margo Irvin, Erica Wetter, Sioned Jones, and Laurie Duboucheix-Saunders; all my colleagues at California State University, Fullerton, especially Dr Jule Selbo, Bob Engels, Ari Posner, Diane Ambruso, Rosanne Welch, and Garrick Dowhen; my colleagues in the Writing Division of the Broadcast Education Association, especially Jon Stahl and Eric Edson; and the reviewers of the initial proposal, Paul Helford, Courtnay McLeod, and two anonymous readers.

1

Introduction and Sample Script

A review of the literature of drama reveals at least eleven broad concepts for a dramatist to consider in any medium, written or performed, on stage or on screen: plot, character, theme, dialogue, sound, spectacle, unity, metaphor, universality, catharsis, and style. To be sure, many texts discuss a variety of additional terms in analyzing drama. However, I posit that those terms have their respective places within these eleven, broader concepts. That is, those additional concepts are derived from the eleven fundamental elements outlined here. The remaining chapters in this book explore each of these concepts in turn. In those chapters, I incorporate many of those additional terms, demonstrating how they are part and parcel of the eleven foundational concepts identified for this introductory primer.

Drama Defined

For this text, the word drama is used with its original Greek meaning: **conflict**. It is not used with the contemporary meaning

Figure 1.1 Drama is conflict, whether "pure" tragedy or comedy, as depicted in these masks, or something between the two

of "serious" or "heavy," as opposed to "comic" or "light," though the Academy of Television Arts and Sciences grants Emmy awards in the categories of "Drama" (usually hour-long episodic television series) and "Comedy" (usually half-hour situation comedies). For this manuscript, all drama is conflict, whether **tragic**, **comic**, or somewhere between the two (see Figure 1.1). In its simplest form, dramatic conflict arises when a person attempts to accomplish something against the obstacles standing in his or her way. The drama ends when the character overcomes the final obstacle, thereby resolving the conflict.

Aristotle and Others

The first recorded exposition of the components of drama is Aristotle's *Poetics* (*c.* 335 BCE). Though Aristotle refers specifically to tragedy in his treatise, the elements apply to all dramatic forms, including comedy (see Chapter 10). Aristotle asserts that dramatic art consists of six elements: plot, character, theme, dialogue, music, and spectacle. Other writers present other typologies. For example, Bailey

Figure 1.2 Aristotle (384–322 BC), the founder of dramatic theory

(1957) lists three components: plot, character, and conflict. Hilliard (2012) discusses seven items: unity, plot, character, dialogue, exposition, preparation, and setting. Winston (1973) offers 16 elements: theme, premise, conflict, crisis-resolution, unity, logic, character, change, foreshadowing, progression, point of attack, point of focus, style, suspense, orchestration, and texture. These are just three examples of the many scholars who divide the elements of drama into useful categories for analysis. All such lists, however, really just condense or expand the elements from Aristotle's typology (Lee 2001). Aristotle still stands today (see Figure 1.2).

In addition to Aristotle's six elements, five other dramatic concepts are found in the literature: unity, metaphor, universality, catharsis, and style. Together, these eleven elements constitute a minimal core of dramatic theory. It is important to note that these components are fully interrelated in drama. While it is useful to separate them for analysis, it is only when they come together in an organic whole that a play is born for the stage or screen. Dialogue cannot happen without the characters who speak it. Style is inseparable from the spectacle that reveals it. Universality does not exist apart from a theme that entices viewers. With this **synergy** of all elements in mind, the chapters that follow explore these foundational elements of drama in turn.

Sample Script: *La Llorona (The Weeping Woman)*

I find it useful in any discussion of drama and story structure to have at least one example of a play or script that everyone reads. While I refer to many plays, movies, and television programs as examples throughout this text, I include here one, short, narrative script as a common reference (see Figure 1.3). I choose this short sample, rather than a feature screenplay, to keep you from getting bogged down. I encourage you to read the following script before proceeding to the remaining chapters. The references to this script throughout the book will then make sense.

The story of *La Llorona* (yo-RO-nah), or *The Weeping Woman*, is a centuries-old story in the Spanish-speaking diaspora. The story is in the public domain. This particular script is my creation, inspired by a video project by one of my students, Ignacio Oliveros, to whom I express my thanks. The script is deliberately short (four pages plus a title page and summary page) for quick reading and reference. The dialogue is deliberately sparse for critique. The story is told more in action than in words because film-video is a visual medium. The characters and settings are described minimally to allow maximum interpretations.

While I hold the copyright to this script, I give my permission for any reader of this book to use it for educational, nonprofit purposes. You may disseminate it for reading and/or production if you do not profit from it. If you produce it, and it turns out so well a distributor wants to buy it, contact me and we'll negotiate a deal!

```
                        LA LLORONA



              An Adaptation of an Old Legend

                       Written by

                     Edward J. Fink
```

© 2014 Edward J. Fink

Figure 1.3 Script of *La Llorona*

Introduction and Sample Script

LA LLORONA

THEME

Primary: Guilt -- remorse serves as its own punishment.
Secondary: Hope -- where there is life, spiritual or physical, there is hope.

LOG LINE

A parent tells a child the legend of a village woman who drowned her twins, losing the bodies in the river, and is doomed to roam the earth searching for her babies.

SYNOPSIS

A CHILD cries out for its mother or father, unable to sleep because of the mournful wind. The PARENT tells the story of "La Llorona." In an old village, an unmarried woman, GUADALUPE, gives birth to TWINS, who are cursed because they have no father. She carries them to the river and drowns them, losing the bodies in the water. She marks a grave but is doomed to roam the earth searching for her babies. As the mother's story ends, the mournful wind dies down, and the child decides that Guadalupe has found her babies at last.

CHARACTERS

Child: either boy or girl, innocent, looks for the good

Parent: either father or mother, comforting, storyteller

Guadalupe: young village woman, troubled with remorse

Village extras, including Old Hag

Figure 1.3 (continued)

```
FADE IN:

INT. BEDROOM — NIGHT

A CHILD sleeps. Perhaps MUSIC plays. The SOUND OF MOURNFUL WIND
is heard. The child's eyes open wide.

                    CHILD
          Mama! Mama! [or Papa! Papa!]

                    PARENT (O.S.)
          Yes, my child, I'm coming.

PARENT enters.

                    PARENT
                  (continuing)
          What is it, sweetheart?

                    CHILD
          The wind, Mama [Papa]. The wind
          sounds strange, like someone is
          crying.

                    PARENT
          Ah, la Llorona.

                    CHILD
          What is la Llorona?

                    PARENT
          La Llorona means "the weeping
          woman." It's an old, old legend.

                    CHILD
          Tell me, Mama [Papa]. Please tell
          me so I can sleep.

The parent settles onto the child's bed.

                    PARENT
          A long time ago, a beautiful woman
          named Guadalupe lived in a village.

EXT. VILLAGE — DAY OR NIGHT

VILLAGERS are gathered around a hut, MUMBLING.
```

Figure 1.3 (continued)

                    PARENT (O.S.)
                    (continuing)
                She had no husband.

SCREAMS OF CHILDBIRTH come from within the hut. An OLD HAG steps
out excitedly. MUSIC PLAYS.

                    OLD HAG
                Twins! Guadalupe has given birth to
                twins. A boy and a girl. But these
                twins are cursed. They have no
                Papa.

The villagers mumble in agreed shame and shunning and then
disperse. The MUSIC builds to a FOREBODING CRESCENDO.

EXT. VILLAGE - DAY

The MUSIC TRANSITIONS to a new day. The hut sits alone. The door
opens. A figure emerges. It is GUADALUPE. She carries a basket,
from which comes the SOUND OF CRYING BABIES.

As she walks through the village, the old hag and the villagers
gather around her, forming a gantlet. They CURSE and HISS at her.
She walks through the crowd to the edge of the village. She keeps
walking.

EXT. RIVER - DAY

Guadalupe walks to the river, alone now. She sets down the basket
and stares at the water. The SOUND OF CRYING BABIES continues
from the basket.

ANGLES ON HER FACE, THE BASKET, THE WATER, PERHAPS THE SKY

Guadalupe begins to HUM A LULLABY. She reaches for the basket,
taking from it two BABIES, wrapped in cloths. She walks slowly
into the water, humming her melody. The BABIES' CRIES SUBSIDE.

Guadalupe takes a breath and submerges herself with her babies.
THE WATER ROILS AND STIRS TO A FRENZY. MUSIC CRESCENDOS.
Guadalupe's head emerges. She remains in the water, submerged to
her neck, straining and shaking violently.
Slowly, she stops shaking, tears streaking down her face. THE
WATER ALSO SETTLES, AS DOES THE MUSIC.

Figure 1.3 (continued)

Guadalupe comes out of the river, her arms empty. She collapses on the riverbank. She sees the basket and picks it up. SHE HEARS THE HAUNTING CRIES OF BABIES. She looks at the river.

She jumps to her feet, drops the basket, and runs back into the water, frantically parting it with her hands, looking, looking. MUSIC BUILDS. She grows hysterical, weeping and flailing about. Beside herself, she SHOUTS TO THE HEAVENS. SILENCE.

Panting, she makes her way out of the water and drops at the river's edge. Exhausted, she reaches for the basket but cannot grasp it. Her head drops. Her hand drops. STILLNESS.

EXT. RIVER - NIGHT

Dressed in a FLOWING GARMENT and a VEIL, Guadalupe, kneeling, finishes pounding a simple, homemade, wooden cross into the ground with a stone. SHE HUMS HER LULLABAY. She leans over, pulls the veil back and kisses the ground.

When she raises her head, her MAKE-UP suggests DEATH AND TEARS.

She removes her veil and drapes it on the cross. She stands and walks away, slowly, mysteriously.

MONTAGE - GUADALUPE WANDERS

She roams through forest and meadow, past river and brook. HAUNTING, SPIRITUAL MUSIC PLAYS.

> PARENT (O.S.)
> To this day, it is said that the
> spirit of Guadalupe wanders the
> earth, searching for her babies.

INT. BEDROOM - NIGHT

The parent is seated on the bed by the child. THE WIND SOBS.

> PARENT
> (continuing)
> And when you hear a sorrowful wind,
> my child, it is the cry of
> Guadalupe.

Figure 1.3 (continued)

                    CHILD
          Do you think she will ever find her
          babies, Mama [Papa]?

                    PARENT
          Ah, that is for each person to
          decide. It is only a story, so you
          can make up your own ending. What
          do you think?

                    CHILD
          Listen, Mama [Papa].

SILENCE. Perhaps a few SOUNDS OF NIGHT.

                    CHILD
                 (continuing)
          The wind has stopped. I think la
          Llorona has found her babies this
          night.

                    PARENT
          And so she has, sweetheart. So she
          has.

The parent strokes the child's cheek, kisses the child and tucks
the child in.

                    CHILD
          Goodnight, Mama [Papa].

                    PARENT
          Goodnight, my child.

The parent stands. MUSIC PLAYS.

ANGLES ON PARENT AND CHILD

The parent exits. MUSIC OUT.

                                                  FADE OUT.

Figure 1.3 (continued)

2

Plot

For Aristotle (c. 335 BCE), **plot** is the most important element of drama (perhaps that's why this is the longest chapter with the most to say). This term is also translated from the Greek **mythos** as "action," "fable," "form," "myth," "story," and "structure." The plot is the arrangement, or sequence, of the action in the story. It is "what happens in the play."

Three-Act Structure

A dramatic plot consists of a beginning, middle, and end. In the broadest sense, this is the three-act structure that makes up much dramatic writing: Act 1 = beginning, Act 2 = middle, Act 3 = end (e.g., Hunter 2004; O'Bannon and Lohr 2012). Interestingly, these three acts are NOT equal in length; each is NOT one-third of the script. In reality, Act 1 is about the first ONE-FOURTH of a script; Act 2 is about the MIDDLE HALF, or TWO-FOURTHS of a script, which can be divided into parts 2A and 2B with the midpoint at the center; Act 3 is the final ONE-FOURTH. Only screenwriters would divide a script into FOUR parts and then call it a THREE-ACT structure. I suppose that's why they're not mathematicians.

Delving deeper, a feature screenplay today is roughly 90–100 pages, with productions running about one minute per page or 90–100 minutes. There are exceptions, of course, such as the longer *The Hobbit* trilogy (Jackson 2012–2014), *Lincoln* (Spielberg 2012), *Skyfall* (Mendes 2012), and others. Note that these films are from A-list directors, however. They have the clout to negotiate **final cut** in their contracts, meaning they have the final say on their films instead of the studio executives, so these directors can create longer films. For beginning and lesser-known writers, as well as established writers working for executives and producers who do not want longer films, 90–100 pages are the norm for a feature script. This means the first Act is about the first 20–25 pages (minutes); the second Act is the middle 50 pages or so (minutes); the third Act is the final 20–25 pages (minutes). These page lengths are guidelines and not absolute rules; however, you'll find if you watch feature films and read screenplays that nearly all films follow this approximate structure.

In short films, the same structure applies, though the page count is obviously less. For a 20-minute film: Act 1 = 5 minutes (pages); Act 2 = 10 minutes (pages; 2A = 5, 2B = 5); Act 3 = 5 minutes (pages). In a four-minute story (e.g., short *animations, webisodes, mobisodes*), as is the case with our sample script, *La Llorona*, the first minute is Act 1, the next two minutes are Acts 2A and 2B, and the last minute is Act 3.

It should be noted that some films, particularly those with lots of action, sometimes have slightly shorter first and third Acts because they have lots of obstacles and characters to deliver in Act 2. One example from comedy-animation is *Finding Nemo* (Stanton and Unkrich 2003). Act 1 quickly sets up the **protagonist**, or main character (see Chapter 3), overprotective father, Clown Fish Marlin (Albert Brooks), and his attempts to keep his son, Nemo (Alexander Gould), at home on the coral reef and safe from the outside world. About one-fifth of the way in (instead of one-fourth), Nemo dares to swim away from the reef to "touch the butt" (boat), when a scuba diver nets him, launching Marlin into the action of Act 2. This Act is a bit longer than just the middle half because of all the characters he meets and obstacles he encounters on his journey: Dory the blue fish with short-term memory loss (his ally), some sharks, a school of fish that does impressions, jellyfish, a 150-year-old turtle, a whale, a seagull, and more. Meanwhile, in the parallel B-story, or **subplot**, through Act 2, Nemo meets many characters and faces many obstacles in the fish tank: Gill the Mastermind, a Pufferfish who bloats when excited, a psycho fish that thinks her reflection is her sister, another psycho fish who is fascinated by bubbles, a starfish who serves as the sentry, and a French shrimp who cleans compulsively. Act 2 ends when the parallel stories come together and Marlin finally sees Nemo in the dentist's office, only to believe Nemo is dead. Act 3 picks up about four-fifths of the way into the story (instead of three-fourths) as a friendly seagull puts the devastated Marlin and Dory back into the harbor to swim home, but wait—Marlin hears Nemo crying out, "Dad," and he's back in the game, moving to the climactic fish fight against the humans, followed by a return to the new normal life back home on the coral reef.

Another example from action-drama is *Speed* (de Bont 1994). Fans of this film remember all the action on the bus as Officer Jack Traven (Keanu Reeves) and Annie Porter (Sandra Bullock) try to keep it from going slower than 50 mph. The bus action is really Act 2. Act 1 finds Traven saving people on an elevator, and Act 3 finds the heroes finally bringing down the **antagonist**, or bad guy (see Chapter 3), Howard Payne (Dennis Hopper) via decapitation on a subway. Here, the first and third Acts are slightly shorter than one-fourth each so the fuller bus action in Act 2 can be a bit longer than one-half.

Exceptions noted, with wiggle room, an average screenplay consists of Act 1 that is about one-fourth, Act 2 that is about the middle half (divided into 2A and 2B at the midpoint), and Act 3 that is about the final fourth. Figure 2.1 illustrates this fundamental three-act structure. Let's look more deeply at the three acts of this diagram. To begin,

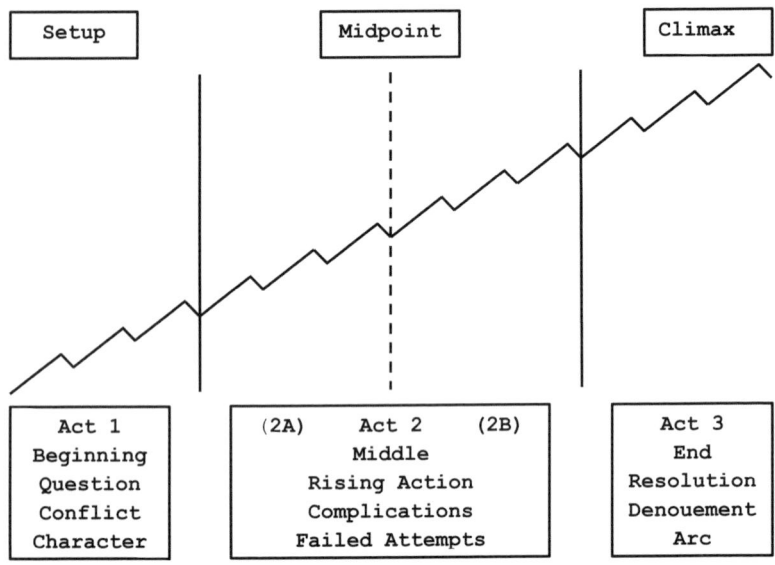

Figure 2.1 Diagram of the fundamental three-act structure, with the linear story progression on the x-axis and the rising tension or action on the y-axis

I use five terms that are integral to a discussion of story on the screen, whether jumbo, large, medium, small, or micro. These terms define the building blocks of structure, from the shortest to the longest in duration.

Some Terms

- **Shot**: The shot is the foundational block of storytelling on the screen (Katz 1991). It is one exposure of the camera. A **close-up** is a shot (head and shoulders), as is a **medium shot** (waist up), a **long shot** (head to toe), and all other shot varieties. A shot might last only a few seconds on the screen before a cut to another shot. For example, if Man A and Woman B are talking in a restaurant, and the camera shows Man A, that is one shot. When the image changes to Woman B,

that is another shot. A shot is analogous to a single word in exposition.
- **Scene**: A scene consists of a number of shots that are in the same time and place. Sometimes a scene plays with no editing among different shots, in which case it is called a **sequence shot**, such as the openings of *Touch of Evil* (Welles 1958) and *The Player* (Altman 1992). Mostly though, a scene consists of multiple shots on the same set or location, consisting of a **master shot** of the entire scene in a **wide shot** and all the **coverage** of that scene, or the different **setups** of tighter shots, such as medium shots and close-ups, all of which are edited together for the final scene. In our example, if Man A and Woman B are talking in a restaurant, all the shots that take place to depict that restaurant conversation make up the restaurant scene. If the actors are next seen at a new time (later) and a new location, say a doorstep, that is a new scene, which consists of all the shots that make up the doorstep scene. A scene is analogous to a sentence in exposition.
- **Sequence**: A sequence is a series of scenes that reveal an overall progression of plot and character. If Man A and Woman B talk in a restaurant scene, and then progress to a more intimate doorstep scene, and then end up in a bedroom scene, that is a sequence of three scenes that shows their progressive attraction to each other, possibly setting up for a falling out when everything starts to unravel. A sequence is analogous to a paragraph in exposition.
- **Act**: An act consists of multiple sequences that constitute the main parts of the story. Act 1 sets up the main characters, their goals, and the main conflict—the **A-story**—while also maybe introducing the **B-story** and maybe even a **C-story** in a feature-length film, though a secondary or tertiary story might be introduced in the second Act, as well. Act 2 begins

when the protagonist is launched into his or her journey, encountering obstacles and conflicts and complications until the **midpoint crisis**—a significant obstacle at the middle of the story that he or she overcomes, thereby recommitting to the journey. That midpoint ends the first half of Act 2, or Act 2A, and is followed by a moment when all seems to go well—the beginning of the second half of Act 2, or Act 2B. From that moment of respite, everything falls apart through the remainder of Act 2, leaving the hero or heroine at his or her absolute lowest point at the end of Act 2. Act 3 begins as something coaxes the protagonist back into action, leading to the ultimate **resolution**, or **climax**, of the story. An act is analogous to a chapter in exposition.

- **Story**: The story is the entire series of events from beginning to end, compromising all three acts and their various sequences, scenes, and shots. A story is analogous to a full manuscript in exposition.

Act 1: Setup to New Direction

A play opens somewhere in space and time. Some call this the **point of attack** (e.g., Smiley 2006; Winston 1973). In many cases, this opening scene is the first scene of the story chronologically. In *Death of a Salesman* (Miller 1949), Willie Loman returns home after a sales trip is cancelled, and from there the dysfunction of his life and relationships run their course to his demise. In *Jurassic Park* (Spielberg 1993), an accident occurs on a remote island involving a mysterious, large, and dangerous creature in a crate, causing the island's owner to call in the expert paleontologists. In some cases, this first chronological scene is actually from the past, revealing something that happened to the protagonist earlier in life that sets the stage for where he or she is today. In *Up* (Docter and Peterson 2009), a young boy in an earlier decade dreams of adventure and meets a girl. This leads to a no-dialogue montage, set to a nostalgic melody, that summarizes their life together from wedding to lost child to her death, thereby setting the stage for the crotchety old man that Carl Fredricksen (Ed Asner) has become. In *The Amazing Spider-Man* (Webb 2012), Peter Parker (Andrew Garfield) appears first as a young boy whose parents must leave quickly, placing him in the care of his aunt and uncle—an opening sequence followed by a jump in time to teenage Parker as he is set up for his quest.

In other cases, the point of attack, or opening scene, takes place later in the story, and then flashes back to the events that led up to this point. In *Forrest Gump* (Zemeckis 1994), the title character (Tom Hanks) is introduced on a bench in Savannah, Georgia, telling his story to another who is waiting for the bus. His life is then told in flashback, occasionally returning to the bench at the end of a segment, only to have him begin telling another segment to a bench newcomer. Eventually, his flashback story catches up to what has brought him to the bench—a letter from his one true love, Jenny Curran (Robin Wright), that she is in Savannah, asking him to visit. From here, he is launched into the remainder of his story in chronological order. In some other cases, the visual sequence is the first chronological scene of the story, but a voice-over from later in the story offers perspective. In *Dances with Wolves* (Costner 1990), we see Lieutenant Dunbar in the Civil War, but after the "suicide ride" sequence, we hear him writing in his diary later in his life about that event and how it set him up for his journey.

The sample script in Chapter 1, *La Llorona*, is an example of a **story-within-a-story**, a **framing structure** that often uses the **bookend** technique, in which the opening and closing are part of a continuous scene. Act 1 opens as a sad-sounding wind keeps a child from sleeping, which brings a parent into the room. The parent tells a story that allows for a transition to another time and place. That story is set up when an unmarried woman, Guadalupe, gives birth to twins at the end of Act 1. Wherever the writer chooses to open Act 1, that first scene is the point of attack for the story, either chronologically, or with a later perspective to which the story eventually catches up, or with an earlier perspective followed by a jump in time to the present.

Early in Act 1 is the **inciting incident** that pulls the protagonist into the story. This is the scene that makes it necessary for the hero to become engaged in this particular drama or comedy. In the previous example of *Jurassic Park*, the opening scene is also the inciting incident—the dinosaur accident is the reason the park owner must persuade experts to come and testify to the park's safety. Likewise in *Jaws* (Spielberg 1975), a girl gets taken by a shark in the opening scene, which soon brings Sheriff Brody (Roy Scheider) into the story. In every television crime drama, a murder—or the discovery of a murder—opens every episode and serves as the inciting incident that brings the cops into the story. While the opening scene is very often also the inciting incident, this is not always the case. Sometimes the inciting incident occurs later in Act 1, after something else has been set up prior to the event that launches the protagonist into action. The film *Witness* (Weir 1985) begins with a relatively long scene among the Pennsylvania Amish, establishing the Amish sense of community and the slow pace of their rustic lifestyle, while also introducing Amish widow Rachel (Kelly McGillis) and her son Samuel (Lukas Haas), who travel by train to the big city. The inciting incident does not occur until they are in the Philadelphia train station, where the Amish boy witnesses a murder in the restroom. This murder brings in the protagonist, homicide detective John Book (Harrison Ford). A number of scenes then establish his character, and Act 1 ends with circumstances conspiring to make him leave Philadelphia and return Rachel and Samuel to their country home. This return to Amish country was set up, of course, in the opening sequence of Amish scenes prior to the inciting incident in the train station restroom.

Following the inciting incident, the remaining scenes of Act 1 reveal the protagonist attempting to solve the problem that has been introduced in a way that is logical for that character (Selbo 2007). This holds true, as well, for characters in the B- and C-stories, if subplots are introduced in Act 1. Back in the A-story, police officers go about the usual police procedures to solve the crime. Doctors follow the usual protocol to cure the disease. Science fiction heroes use their usual weapons to kill the monster aliens. Of course, these usual or logical attempts all fail. If they worked, there would be no story. Instead, the principal characters have to abandon their usual methods at the end of Act 1 and try something different.

They are forced out of their comfort zones into new territory because Act 1 ends with a significant obstacle that the protagonist did not see coming, and which now forces him or her to turn in a new direction, launching the start of the journey—the quest. This major obstacle is **plot point one**, the first **subclimax** and major **turnaround**: Often this quest involves physically leaving home to go out and accomplish what needs to be done. In the example of *Witness*, Book learns in Act 1 that the murder is an inside job within the police department, and at the end of the Act, he is shot by the murdering cop himself. Realizing that this goes all the way to the top, Book has to flee with the mother and boy to save the boy's life. In the example of *La Llorona*, Guadalupe has her babies, but because they are bastard children, she must leave the taunting villagers at the end of Act 1 to do what she thinks will right this wrong. She launches her journey by heading to the river.

Act 2A: Launch of Journey to Midpoint Crisis

Act 2 begins as the hero or heroine sets out on his or her quest. The journey begins. After the high action subclimax that ends Act 1, the first scene of Act 2 usually allows a moment of respite from the action, slowing things briefly for the audience to collect its breath as the protagonist collects his or her breath for the road ahead. The road metaphor is useful because the first scene of Act 2 often shows the protagonist literally on a road of some kind as he or she moves to the next point of tension. Continuing our examples, in *Witness*, Book drives Rachel and Samuel to their Amish home in Lancaster County. In *La Llorona*, a new day dawns as Guadalupe emerges from her hut with her twins in a basket and walks through the village (her path or road). In another example, *Star Wars* (Lucas 1977), Luke Skywalker (Mark Hamill), having discovered his burned home and murdered aunt and uncle at the end of Act 1, commits to his crusade and sets off. In a similar vein in *Gladiator* (Scott 2000), Maximus (Russell Crowe) hurries home at the end of Act 1 only to find his wife and son murdered, causing him to faint from grief and exhaustion. Act 2 begins as he awakens, picked up by slave traders who take him on the road (literally) to his destiny.

It is important to note that the quest does not always begin on the road to somewhere new, though that is often the case. In intimate character dramas and comedies, the main character sometimes goes on his or her journey of self-discovery without actually wandering far from home. For example, in *Casablanca* (Curtiz 1942), Rick Blaine (Humphrey Bogart) does not wander too far from his "gin joint"; yet, he undergoes a journey that rekindles a passion and reconnects him to what is important in life. In a less well-known film, but a personal favorite of mine, *Waking Ned Devine* (Jones 1998), Jackie O'Shea (Ian Bannen) discovers in Act 1 that a local man in his Irish village has won the lottery but died from the excitement of it. He engages in a quest to collect the lottery money all the same, and his journey takes him around the village, but not on the road to anywhere new.

Still, while stories such as these do not send the hero literally on a trip to another land, Act 2 begins all the same with the protagonist entering unfamiliar territory. This is necessary to move the story along and keep it interesting. The hero has to encounter these unfamiliar obstacles or the story would lag. In *Casablanca*, Blaine, who has run from his past and hardened his heart, learns at the start of Act 2 that Nazi underground resistance leader Victor Laszlo has arrived in Casablanca with a woman who turns out to be a past love. Blaine discovers that he has feelings again, and he is conflicted about what to do with them. In *Waking Ned Devine*, Act 2 begins with Jackie O'Shea walking to the dead man's house with a friend ("on the road" so to speak, though in the same village), entering the unfamiliar territory of what to do with a corpse and how to claim its lotto winnings.

Throughout Act 2A, the protagonist continues to attempt to resolve the problem that has been thrust upon him or her, but continues to fail, though he or she is learning new lessons and skills through these trials—lessons and skills that he or she will need later for the final showdown. **Tension** rises at each failed attempt, and then releases, building up again to the next failed attempt, or **plot point**. This is **rising action**, which carries throughout all the Acts, not just Act 2, as diagrammed in Figure 2.1. I mention this "ebb and flow" nature of scriptwriting here, though, because it is in Act 2, the center half of the story, that it is really important to take the viewers on a ride up and down hills and around curves to keep them engaged. The rise and release of tension provides the rhythm of the story, and that rhythm holds audience attention. This rise and fall of action is similar to a roller coaster ride, which has the riders holding onto their seats for life, then releases the tension so they can breathe, only to build the tension again, and so on. Action films are a good example because they sometimes feel like roller coaster rides with their strategically-placed action scenes. However, all dramatic stories have this rise and fall of tension, including dramas and comedies, even if the tension is more in emotion and dialogue than in physical action.

The failed attempts at resolution in the unfamiliar territory of Act 2A ultimately lead to the middle point of the story. Here is where the midpoint crisis occurs. This **midpoint ordeal** is the biggest obstacle the protagonist has faced so far. This time, though, he or she is successful. The protagonist finally wins a battle, though not yet the war (final victory must wait for the end). This ordeal can be a literal battle, of course, but it can also be something else. It might be a big scene with action. For example, in *Star Wars*, Luke and friends escape the trash compactor. In *La Llorona*, Guadalupe drowns her babies. However, the midpoint can also be a smaller scene—a psychological or emotional crisis with little or no physical action. In *Witness*, Book commits to stay with the Amish for a while and help out on the farm. In *Casablanca*, Blaine flashes back to his affair with Ilsa in Paris.

Whatever the obstacle at the middle of the story, physical or psychological (usually both), big or small, a strong **midpoint** accomplishes five things. First, it provides a significant crisis point to keep the story engaging. Keep in mind that tension builds and releases throughout a story, so the midpoint ordeal provides an excellent plot point to build tension. Second, it is important for the protagonist to experience a triumph half-way through. If a person always loses when trying to accomplish a goal, eventually that person gives up. In storytelling, the main character (and other principals in B- and C-stories, too) have to claim a victory at the midpoint so they can recommit to the journey. There is no more turning back. The audience also re-engages in the story at this point (and hopefully also does not turn back by going home or turning off the TV).

Third, the midpoint moves the protagonist half-way along his or her **arc**—the change he or she undergoes as a result of the journey. In *Witness*, Book learns more about the Amish ways of non-violence and community. He is not yet at the end of his arc, as seen by his punching a tourist at the end of Act 2B, but he is on his way to giving non-violence a chance. In *La Llorona*, Guadalupe demonstrates her resoluteness, even if the demonstration is the unthinkable act of drowning her babies. She is not yet at the end of her arc, as seen by her turn back into the river to find the babies' bodies, but she is on her way to the total resolve that becomes her destiny. In *Casablanca*, Blaine is learning to feel again. He is not yet ready to commit to the Nazi resistance, but the shell he has put around his heart is cracking.

Fourth, the midpoint **foreshadows** the ending climax. In *Star Wars*, Skywalker's trash compacter experience foreshadows his flying through crushing obstacles for the final battle and explosion of the Death Star. In *Witness*, Book's committing to stay and help the Amish predicts the end when he stands with his Amish friends and persuades the bad guy to drop the shotgun and kill no more. In *La Llorona*, Guadalupe's death of her children points to the end when she herself is dead or dead-like, suffering her mournful fate. In yet another example, *Kung Fu Panda* (Osborne and Stevenson 2008), Po (Jack Black) overcomes his inability to learn the Kung Fu ways at the midpoint when his master discovers that he can use food to train Po, and the two have an extended chopstick sequence. This foreshadows the end when Po dons bamboo trunks as stilts and does final battle, chopstick style, with the evil leopard.

Fifth, the midpoint sets up a moment of "all goes well" (Selbo 2007), which begins the second half of Act 2, Act 2B. By overcoming the midpoint ordeal, which ends Act 2A, the protagonist is rewarded, if only for a short time, at the start of Act 2B. Structurally, this moment of respite is necessary to release the tension from the midpoint crisis as the protagonist and the audience re-engage in the story, setting things up for the fall that is the second half of Act 2.

Act 2B: All Goes Well to All Is Lost

The second half of the second Act begins as the protagonist recovers from his or her successful triumph over the midpoint ordeal and enjoys a brief moment of victory, along with the audience. The tension eases as everyone enters the second half of the story, preparing for the build-up to the great tension of the hero's or heroine's lowest point that is to come at the end of Act 2. In *Kung Fu Panda*, Po's training goes well for a little while. In *Witness*, Book assists on the farm by milking cows and using his carpentry skills to fix the birdhouse into which he inadvertently crashed his car (the birdhouse being a metaphor for what he has broken and must fix).

This "all goes well" or "reward" sequence can be longer or shorter, depending on the needs of the story. Selbo (2007) notes that the genre often dictates the relative length of this part of the play. For example, romantic comedies tend to have a longer respite as the lovers finally get together. They need a break half-way through to entice them to stay in the game of love that has been nothing but trouble so far. The audience, too, enjoys seeing the happy couple as the second half of the story gets underway. Inevitably though, the happy moment or moments give way to another obstacle that ends the respite, tears the couple apart, and plunges them to their lowest points at the end of Act 2.

In contrast, action-adventure stories usually have a very short "all goes well" moment at the beginning of Act 2B. A shorter respite is necessary so the protagonist is taken quickly "out of the frying pan into the fire." This genre is heavy on action, after all, so the moments of relief are briefer by design so that more time can be spent on action.

Often the "all goes well" sequence is a **montage** of various scenes set to music. In a generic example common to many romantic comedies, the lovers walk through the park, get ice cream, go out on a lake in a canoe, run through a rainstorm, giggle and kiss, and so on, while a romantic string melody plays throughout. In a generic action-adventure example, a series of shots show the hero building a new gadget or bulking up in preparation for the final showdown, while heart-pumping rhythms play. While not all films have musical montages at the start of the second half of the story, these montages are a useful way to show passages of time while the protagonist enjoys the fruit of his or her labors momentarily, while also moving the principal characters along their arcs. Whether a musical montage or a series of scenes or a single scene, Act 2B begins with a moment of relative calm to prepare the characters and audience alike for the downfall that follows.

Once the hero has had his or her brief moment of reward, something inevitably goes bad and the pleasantness ends. The protagonist faces another challenge that he is not yet prepared to overcome. Perhaps the bad guy resurfaces. In *Witness*, Book's partner back in Philadelphia is shaken down by the cops; Book's troubles are not yet over in Amish country. In *Up*, the nice dinner with Carl's childhood hero, Charles Muntz (Christopher Plummer) turns bad when Carl realizes that his hero is up to no good, trying to capture the last member of a rare bird species. In *La Llorona*, having exited the river and collapsed for a brief moment to rest, Guadalupe must rush back in to try to find her dead babies.

More obstacles and challenges abound through the remainder of Act 2, each one more serious than the previous. Action continues to rise and fall, with each new level of tension being higher than the one before, as diagrammed in Figure 2.1. Each problem must be bigger than the one before it so that the protagonist is worn down more and more, logically resulting in his or her lowest point at the end of Act 2. McKee (2010) notes: "A story must not retreat to actions of lesser quality or magnitude, but move progressively forward to a final action beyond which the audience cannot imagine another" (209). To accomplish this, the **stakes** must be raised with each ordeal.

Metaphorically, it is useful to think of escalating weapons. The sequence is "sticks → knives → guns." That does not mean that three things happen, one with a stick, then one with a knife, and then one with a gun, though that could be the case. Rather, the metaphor of escalating weapons means that, however many scenes make up Act 2B, the challenges have greater stakes. Don't go with the gun first, and then backtrack to knives and sticks. That would be anti-climactic. Start with the smaller weapons (obstacles) and work up, all the time remembering that each weapon still harms the hero and keeps him or her from reaching the end.

Act 2 ends with major **plot point two**, the second subclimax and major turnaround: another significant obstacle that the protagonist did not see coming, and that now thrusts him or her down to his or her lowest possible point. He or she has faced escalating crises and has failed. The hero has used everything in his or her box of tools and has nothing left. The last rug has been pulled out from under him or her—each "rug" being a metaphor for a reason to hope. All hope is lost. It is the hero's darkest hour. Try as he or she might, the protagonist has lost the fight and can hold out no longer. There is nothing left. He or she might as well just lie down and die. In *Witness*, Book learns in a telephone call that his partner has been murdered. His one hope in the corrupt police department is gone. In *Up*, Carl chooses to save his house from fire rather than save the rare bird from the bad guy. It seems death will result from his inability to let his house go—his past life with his wife. In *Finding Nemo*, Marlin finally arrives at the dentist's office to see his son Nemo, only to believe he is dead. The one thing that has carried him through all his trials has been the hope of saving his son, and now that hope is gone—or so he believes. In *La Llorona*, Guadalupe cannot find her twins' dead bodies in the river. She has nothing. Here ends Act 2.

Act 3: Turnaround to Climax and Denouement

Act 3 begins with a plot turnaround. Something happens that sets the story in a new direction. Specifically, this turnaround pulls the protagonist back from the abyss and propels him or her back into action. Act 2 ends with the protagonist at his or her lowest point, with all hope lost, ready to die. How awful if the story were to end there. We want him or her to get back up and storm the castle (metaphorically and sometimes literally). We are only satisfied if our hero finishes the quest. The third Act, then, must begin with a **spark** of some kind that brings the hero or heroine from the lowest point back to life.

That spark can be many things. Sometimes the mentor figure appears. In George Lucas's *Star Wars* (1977), Obi-Wan Kenobi's voice (Alec Guinness) comes to Luke to remind him to "use the force." Sometimes the protagonist discovers something he or she had set aside, maybe in a pocket or on a table. In many romantic comedies, the hero sees a photo of his or her loved one and, realizing that true love is worth the battle, gets up and heads out into Act 3. Other times the protagonist has something inside himself or herself that does the trick. In *Up*, the boy Russell takes off with some balloons to save the rare bird, and Carl feels his responsibility to save the boy above all, even above the house. In *Witness*, Book connects with Rachel in the rain and his love for her and fatherly instinct to protect Samuel propels him to face the bad guys who arrive the next morning. In *Finding Nemo*, a friendly pelican delivers a devastated Marlin and Dory back to the harbor; Marlin takes his leave from Dory and swims away; but soon he hears Nemo's voice. His son is alive! He's back in the quest! With his son by his side, he is ready to face anything, even the ultimate bad guys—the human fishermen (foreshadowed at the end of Act 1 by the human diver-dentist who took Nemo).

Act 3 progresses from the turnaround through a few more challenges—more in longer stories, fewer in shorter ones—until the finish line: the **climax**. The climax is the final resolution of the story. Some climactic scenes take longer to play out than others, again depending on the needs of the story and the genre. Action-adventure films have long climaxes with lots of action because the climactic scene has to be the biggest of them all. It is the scene that pays off the viewers for sticking with the story for about two hours. Comedies might have shorter climaxes because no one really ends up permanently harmed (see Chapter 10). However long the final battle (either literal or metaphoric), the climactic moment occurs when the protagonist finally defeats the antagonist.

In **tragedy**, the protagonist faces ruin as he or she defeats the bad guy. In *Oedipus Rex*, Oedipus discovers that he himself is the reason for the curse on Thebes and blinds himself with his wife's/mother's broach (see Chapter 5, Figure 5.1). In *Gladiator*, Maximus defeats Commodus, but dies himself at the end of the battle. In *La Llorona*, Guadalupe enters her judgment, wandering the earth in a never-ending search for the children she murdered.

In **melodrama**—the genre known more simply today as "drama"—the protagonist is not ruined, but the ending is still serious rather than comic in tone. In *Witness*, the final shoot-out on the Amish farm (a lengthy climax) ends with Book blowing away two bad cops before finally cornering the last and highest-ranking one. Surrounded by Amish, Book persuades him to drop his weapon. There has been enough killing.

In comedy, the ending is always happy. In the comedy-adventure *Finding Nemo*, Marlin urges his son on as Nemo coaches the fish trapped in the net to "swim down," ultimately tearing the man-made net and freeing the fish. In *Up*, Carl ultimately defeats the evil Muntz as Muntz falls from the blimp (with a few balloons attached so maybe he'll land OK, but still defeated—we don't want to frighten the children with a gruesome death). All is well at the end of comedy.

While the climax is the final resolution of the story, the story does not quite end there. After the protagonist has learned the lessons and gained the strength and skills needed to overcome the final climactic struggle and win the day (whether the protagonist himself or herself lives happily ever after or not), the characters—and audience—need a moment to breathe and regroup after the final battle. Additionally, we want to see how the world has changed because of this story. We want to glimpse the "new normal" of our heroes and heroines before leaving the theater or turning off the TV feeling satisfied (cathartically purged—see Chapter 9). This "moment after" the climax is the **denouement**: the brief last scene or scenes of the play. In *Gladiator*, after Maximus dies, a good Senator takes over the leadership of Rome so we know that this great state will continue, and in the afterlife, Maximus reunites at last with his wife and son—all he ever really wanted. In *Witness*, Book leaves the Amish a changed man, and one of the Amish men walks down the lane to Rachel's farm so she and her son will be all right, too. In *Up*, Carl has returned home, but now he enjoys life as Russell's adopted grandfather. In *Finding Nemo*, Marlin and Nemo are back home on the barrier reef with all the colorful characters who made the journey so engaging. In *La Llorona*, the child in the present day decides that Guadalupe has finally found her children and can rest, now that the wind has quieted.

Throughout all Three Acts

Having analyzed each of the three acts in the three-act structure, some additional concepts are important to the study of dramatic writing—concepts that occur throughout all three acts. The primary ingredient of an interesting plot is **suspense**. That does not mean a literal **cliffhanger**, though that is one type of suspense. Rather, suspense refers to some element/s in the plot that make/s the audience want to watch the play until the end (e.g., Smiley 2006). Some ingredient is planted early and periodically throughout the story—a setup that leaves the viewers wondering what will happen next. In the end, the viewers receive a **payoff** when all the plot ingredients come together and all the questions are answered—all the conflicts are resolved. In *La Llorona*, the baby twins provide the suspense as the viewers watch to see their fate unfold, and consequently the fate of their mother. Many authors offer deeper examinations of plot, including the top-selling Syd Field (2005) and others (e.g., Lucey 1996; Miller 1997; Stempel 1982).

A screenplay tells its story through two vehicles: **action** and **dialogue**. The play is a blueprint for production, so all the story and character points must be revealed in what happens on the screen or stage and what people say. Unlike writing a novel or short story, in which the author can describe a character's inner thoughts and feelings, in a play those inner ideas and emotions cannot be described for the readers to read because, after all, no one outside of the production reads the screenplay. Rather, the audience watches the finished product. To reveal inner thoughts, the characters must engage in action and/or speak words that demonstrate what is inside their minds and hearts. Of course, those actions and dialogue can be a literal statement of the character's motivation at that moment, or they can be different actions and dialogue, relying on **subtext** to reveal what is really happening (see Chapter 5). Consider the words, "I love you." Those can be literal, say, at the end of a romance film when one partner realizes he or she really does the lover the other, after all. However, those same words can mean the opposite, "I hate you," if spoken sarcastically after a heated fight between lovers. Part of the art of writing is creating scenes with context that gives clues to the actors regarding what their words and actions really mean. Character and dialogue are covered in greater depth in Chapters 3 and 4; I only touch on them here because characters drive plot, and their dialogue and action are the vehicles to do that.

Throughout the play, **exposition** occurs in dialogue and action that reveals who the characters are and why and how they came into conflict. This **back story**—the things that happened prior to the point of attack that the audience needs to learn to understand the characters' motivations and actions—is uncovered as the characters move through the three acts. Each dramatic **beat** signifies a point in the story's structure that sets something in motion that leads to another beat throughout the story.

The key to building suspense, revealing back story, and so on is to create **complications** in action and dialogue throughout the story. These complications can be external or internal to the character, and are often both. They serve as roadblocks and detours on the protagonist's path to solving the conflict. He or she must go over or under or around these obstacles (avoid, adapt, or triumph) to arrive at the final destination, and the story happens in confronting those obstacles, often unsuccessfully with occasional successes to move the story forward. What kind of story would *The Wizard of Oz* be if Dorothy tells the Munchkins she would like to return to Kansas and they say, "OK, walk over there and you'll be home"?

Or how satisfied would you feel if Glinda the Good Witch, upon seeing that Dorothy's house landed on the Wicked Witch's sister, said at this point, "Click your heels three times and say, 'There's no place like home,'" and Dorothy was back home, having never met the scarecrow, tin man, or lion, and having never gone to Oz? Or what if Dorothy made it all the way to Oz, announced she would like to go home, and the Wizard simply said "OK" instead of sending her to retrieve the evil witch's broomstick? Neither of those scenarios makes for much of a story. It is in the complications along the way and in meeting interesting characters that a real story unfolds.

One more example drives these points home. The American Film Institute has voted *Citizen Kane* (Welles 1941) the greatest film of cinema's first 100 years. In the plot of this classic, a reporter sets out to find the meaning of Charles Foster Kane's (Orson Welles) dying word, "Rosebud." The point of attack—where the movie opens—is actually a point in time near the end of the linear story—the moment when the elder Kane utters the word and dies. Throughout the plot, the **flashback** technique is used as the journalist uncovers one piece of evidence at a time about Kane's character and back story—sometimes called **peeling the onion** one layer at a time. Rising action, tension, and suspense build as the viewers—and the reporter—hang on to learn the significance of Rosebud. In the end, the reporter is unsuccessful at unraveling the mystery, but the final shot (denouement) pays off the audience by revealing Rosebud to the viewers.

Experiments with Three-Act Structure

It is important to note that some dramatists experiment with these conventional notions of plot. Some argue against the three-act structure, asserting more acts, such as the traditional four-act structure of episodic TV drama—which is now five acts with an additional commercial pod—or the five-act structure of Shakespearean drama, or the seven-act structure of movies of the week. Some note fewer acts, such as the two-act structure of some sitcoms or musicals with intermissions. Some posit no acts at all, such as the converging but out-of-sequence plots of *Pulp Fiction* (Tarantino 1994) or the backwards plot of *Memento* (Nolan 2000). These are all valid arguments regarding the formal designation of acts within each stage- or tele- or screenplay.

For this general primer, however, the conventional three-act structure is presented in its broadest sense, meaning that every story, no matter how many formal acts or lack of acts the writer plots out, whether forwards or backwards or jumping through time and space, the story starts somewhere (beginning), goes somewhere (middle), and ends somewhere (end). In this sense, a five-act TV drama has its beginning (Act 1), its middle (Acts 2, 3, and 4), and its end (Act 5): the five acts are simply designated in commercial American television because the story is traditionally interrupted four times for advertisements, making five segments.

Likewise, Shakespeare's plays, while formally structured in five acts as well, still begin, progress through a middle, and then end (here, too, the middle typically consists of Acts 2, 3, and 4). A seven-act movie of the week also has the three basic parts (Acts 2 through 6 often make up the middle). Similarly, a two-act musical, say *The Sound of Music* (Wise 1965), starts somewhere (a conflicted nun sings on a hillside while an aristocrat seeks a new nanny), progresses through beats and plot points and turnarounds and subclimaxes (she gets the nanny job, falls in love with the aristocrat, who is betrothed to another, so she leaves, but comes back at the children's pleading, then he breaks the engagement, all the while Nazis bear down, etc.), and ends with the resolution (they marry and escape the Nazis by fleeing into the hills where the point of attack began the story hours earlier).

Even *Pulp Fiction* has a beginning, middle, and end. The scenes are arranged outside the usual chronological order, so the movie begins with a scene that is actually close to the end of converging storylines. However, an editor could rearrange all the scenes in chronological order to reveal that each plot line does, in fact, have a beginning, middle, and end. Tarantino simply scrambles the sequence. Ditto *Memento*, which could be re-edited in reverse order to create a traditional linear story (but a very different film).

Some dramatists even experiment with no plot at all. For example, *Waiting for Godot* (Beckett 1953) ends exactly where it begins, with two bumpkins on a deserted road waiting for someone who will never arrive. This lack of apparent plot progression underscores the futility of the characters' existence. Yet, the play—like all plays—begins somewhere, and something happens in the middle, though the action and dialogue seem purposely trivial and futile, and the play eventually ends. There are beginning, middle, and end, so there is a plot of sorts. It is Beckett's playing with this structure, having the end return to the beginning with no character progression during the middle, that makes the existential point of the play.

Sample Plot Points

This chapter has covered the fundamental elements of plot, while also introducing some other concepts necessary to discuss storylines. These elements are derived from myriad texts about dramatic writing. Each manuscript approaches story in a unique way. This book pulls together the main ideas about which those other books agree. Noting that, many texts are authored by writing "gurus": individuals who have developed a method for screenwriting that works for them, so they share those methods in their books. Each of them is a worthwhile read, and I recommend those texts to anyone who wishes to write for the screen and also the stage. You might also find Dramatica or other software programs useful in creating your stories. These programs can assist you in writing characters whose decisions drive the story points.

Here, allow me to summarize a sample of three different gurus' approaches to story. There are more, but these three serve to illustrate how the myriad authors of screenwriting texts agree on the basics (similarities) while explicating their own views (differences). Each one lays out a different number of "steps," but they all generally follow the three-act structure: beginning (opening 1/4th), middle (central 2/4th), and end (closing 1/4th). The difference among the gurus is that each breaks down each act into greater or fewer steps, depending on the objectives of his or her writing. Some are more interested in the broader brushstrokes and discuss what must happen in each act more qualitatively than in specific, quantitative steps, such as the popular books by Field (2005), Hunter (2004), and Seger (2010). Others conduct a more scene-by-scene analysis and break out each act into more quantitative steps. As examples, let us compare the different steps of three scholars. It must be noted that the outlines that follow are over-simplifications of these authors' works. These outlines are useful for comparison; however, each step has much more than is suggested by the few key words listed here. I recommend reading these books in their entirety to grasp all that happens at each step.

Jule Selbo's 11 Steps (2007)

Selbo's 11 story points stem from the character's motivation, need, or want at each point. Selbo usefully distinguishes between a character's immediate goal and overall want. The goal is what the person thinks he or she needs to do now (e.g., solve the murder). The want is a psychological or emotional need the character longs to fulfill (e.g., find true love), even though he or she may or may not know that at the beginning and only achieves it at the end.

Act 1

1. Character's want-need is established, and why.
2. Character logically goes for it.
3. Character is denied.

Act 2A

4. Character gets second opportunity.
5. Character experiences conflicts about taking advantage of second opportunity: moral, emotional, physical.
6. Character goes for it.

Act 2B

7. All goes well.
8. All falls apart.
9. Conflict rises or descends to a crisis point.

Act 3

10. Conflict intensifies to create final climax.
11. Truth comes out (resolution).

Here it is clear how these eleven steps align with the three acts. Some would argue that this simplification of steps looks as if the climax (step 10) is the first part of Act 3, which is not the case. The climax is at the end, just before the denouement. It must be noted that Selbo does explicate Act 3 in great detail in her book, making it clear that the climax does not occur immediately in Act 3, but that it follows step 9. Moreover, step 9 is where the protagonist must decide whether or not to go forward into Act 3. This is an example of the importance of reading the primary texts that I summarize here. These summaries necessarily only serve to illustrate the points of similarities and differences among authors.

Chris Vogler's 12 Steps (2007), based on Campbell (1949)

Vogler calls his steps "stages of the journey." He diagrams these stages in a circle to show that the hero leaves his or her "ordinary world" in Act 1 (quadrant 1), entering and moving through the "special world" in Act 2 (quadrant 2 = 2A, quadrant 3 = 2B), and returning home to the "ordinary world" in Act 3 (quadrant 4). The characters whom the hero meets are mythological types: "mentor," "threshold guardian," "herald," "shapeshifter," "shadow," "ally," and "trickster."

Act 1: Separation

1. Ordinary world: limited awareness of problem.
2. Call to adventure: increased awareness.
3. Refusal of the call: reluctance to change.
4. Meeting with the mentor: overcoming reluctance.

Act 2A: Descent

5. Crossing the first threshold: committing to change.
6. Tests, allies, enemies: experimenting with the first change.
7. Approach to the inmost cave: preparing for big change.
8. Ordeal: attempting big change [midpoint].

Act 2B: Initiation

9. Reward (seizing the sword): consequences of the attempt (improvements and setbacks).

Act 3: Return

10. The road back: rededication to change.
11. Resurrection: final attempt at big change.
12. Return with the elixir: final mastery of the problem.

Here some would say Act 2B is too thin with just one step—9. As with Selbo (and Edson who follows), it is important to read the full text. Vogler explicates each step to demonstrate much more than is summarized here. It is important to note that Vogler bases these steps on the work of scholar Joseph Campbell (1949), who devoted his professional life to the study of myths and legends around the world.

Campbell discovered that all myths, in whatever culture they develop, share certain characteristics common to all hero stories. Among these are similar stages along the journey that make these legends engaging, meaningful, and timeless. Vogler adapts these mythological stages to the stages of a screenplay.

Eric Edson's 23 Steps (2011)

Edson calls his steps "hero goal sequences" (HGS). His definition:

A Hero Goal Sequence consists of three to seven pages of screenplay—usually two to four scenes—wherein the hero pursues one short-term physical goal as a step toward achieving ultimate victory in the story. Then the hero discovers some form of new information I call Fresh News that brings the current goal to an end and presents a new short-term physical goal—thereby launching the next Hero Goal Sequence (155).

Edson notes that there is some play, or wiggle room, among these sequences. For example, the inciting incident can occur at different steps, as long as it is early, say steps 1–3. Likewise, the climax can occur at, say, step 20 or 21 or 22, as long as it is before the denouement, which is the next and final step (21 or 22 or 23 if the climax is 20, 21, or 22, respectively). "Action bursts" can occur in the sequences noted below, or perhaps one sequence earlier or later, though always after a quieter moment so that the new action re-engages characters and audience in the story (this is the rise and fall of tension). Additionally, different characters can appear in different sequences throughout. Most notably, the adversary must appear early for his or her actions to drive conflict, and the mentor or mentors must appear when the hero needs advice or tools (or both) to move forward. The steps are (emphasis added on certain steps):

Act 1

1. Introduction of hero, including everyday life, inner turmoil, and shield of self-defense.
2. Introduction of central conflict with adversary: often, but not always, inciting incident.
3. Call to adventure; love interest might appear; adversary sets trap for hero.
4. Hero takes risk; steps into trap; new characters appear (e.g., mentor).
5. Revelation of hero's desire; second thoughts; refusal of call; possible meeting with adversary.
6. *Stunning surprise #1;* trap is shut; goal is clear for Act 2.

Act 2A

7. Hero flounders for a plan; commits to journey; inner conflict reveals theme.
8. Adversary displays great strength; hero undergoes training; *first step of character growth—hero expresses inner emotional turmoil.*
9. *First action burst—high energy or emotion that drives up tension;* hero takes a risk that backfires.
10. Hero gets a setback; possibly consults new mentor.
11. Hero approaches adversary's inmost cave; prepares to fight; last chance to train and consult mentor.
12. Midpoint: point of no return—no turning back; conflict with adversary becomes personal; *second step of character growth—hero battles inner emotional turmoil.*

Act 2B

13. Hero presses onward toward goal; lifts shield of self-defense.
14. New idea appears as hero contemplates; love interest or sidekick brings up inner conflict issues with which hero does not want to deal.

15. *Second action burst of high energy or emotion*; fleeting sense of security.
16. Hero feels greater confidence; *third step of character growth—hero overcomes inner emotional turmoil.*
17. Adversary displays great strength again, this time personal; hero makes final preparations for showdown.
18. *Stunning surprise #2*; biggest reversal, peak of conflict so far, but not final resolution.

Act 3 (total sequences might be minimum 20, max 23)

19. Hero "rises from the dead" (literally or figuratively), required by ending of Act 2.
20. Might be obligatory scene (climax), or might be more obstacles on the way.
21. Might be obligatory scene (climax), or might be more obstacles or subplot resolution.
22. Obligatory scene for sure (climax, payoff).
23. Denouement: wrap-up shows equilibrium returned to hero's ordinary world.

With this final example, we see both differences and similarities. The differences are in the number of steps each author discusses per act. The similarities are the three-act structure, with the story divided into roughly-equal fourths, and with Act 2 comprising the two middle fourths, Act 2A and Act 2B. There is agreement that Act 1 sets up characters and conflicts, ending with a major plot point, or turnaround, or "stunning surprise." This causes the protagonist to launch unprepared into unfamiliar territory at the start of Act 2A, floundering for a plan, facing obstacles, meeting new characters, and growing to a midpoint at the end of Act 2A from which there is no turning back. The hero overcomes the midpoint obstacle and is rewarded for a brief moment at the beginning of Act 2B, allowing him or her to press on, encountering more trials and tribulations, and facing another major plot point-turnaround-stunning surprise that brings him or her down to the lowest point at the end of Act 2B. Act 3 begins with "rising from the dead," or finding a reason to get back in the race, and heading toward the finish line, doing final battle with the antagonist in the "obligatory scene," or climax, followed by the denouement.

Summary

This chapter has explored the Aristotelian element of *plot* and its foundational elements and concepts. The *three-act structure* is the overarching frame of any story. Many scholars have analyzed this structure, both qualitatively and quantitatively. Some have been summarized here. While different authors offer different approaches to story structure, it is possible to derive commonalities among them. This common ground constitutes the fundamental principles of story structure.

Having posited a general diagram of plot at the start of this chapter (Figure 2.1), including **act breaks**, **rising action**, moments of **tension** and **relief**, and so on, I offer here a summary breakdown of the three-act structure. Each part of each act might require more or fewer **scenes** or *steps*, depending on the needs of the story and character development. **Tension** might ebb and flow at different times, all the while **rising upward** to **greater stakes**. New *characters* might appear in different places to help or hinder the *hero*, often changing as the story progresses: a supposed *ally* becomes an *enemy* and a supposed enemy turns out to be an ally. The *B-story* and *C-story* scenes might come in at different places, but always in support of the *A-story*. That is, if a B-story character overcomes a major *obstacle*, that occurs adjacent to the A-story protagonist overcoming an obstacle; if a C-story *moment of respite* is needed, that occurs adjacent to a similar A-story moment of respite; and so on. These choices are the skill and art of dramatic writing. The framework on which these creative choices are fastened, however, follows these summary dimensions of the three-act structure:

Act 1: Setup to new direction—establish characters needs/wants and conflict

1. Establish world and main character's wants and needs.
2. Inciting incident that causes hero to go into action.
3. Plot point one, subclimax of Act 1: main character must change original direction.

Act 2A: Launch of journey to midpoint crisis—obstacles and unsuccessful attempts

4. Launch into journey to face obstacles: hero strives for goal, encounters obstacles, faces surprises, unresolved conflict.
5. Obstacles, conflicts, complications, escalation, rising action.
6. Midpoint: big challenge that protagonist overcomes.

Act 2B: All goes well to all is lost—progression from reward to lowest point

7. All goes well momentarily for hero as reward for overcoming midpoint crisis.
8. All falls apart with new or recurring obstacles, conflicts, complications, escalation, rising action.
9. Plot point two, subclimax of Act 2: major crisis that brings protagonist to lowest point.

Act 3: Turnaround to climax and denouement—push to resolution and order restored

10. Turnaround: hero gets his mojo back, heads on the path to resolution, with some obstacles yet before the finish (more or less, depending on story, character, and genre).
11. Plot point three: climax of movie, highest tension, biggest scene, protagonist finally defeats antagonist (both external and internal), conflict is resolved.

12. Denouement: sense that character is on new path and there is a future; equilibrium restored to new normal world.

This progression holds up for all genres and lengths of drama, with some points lasting longer with more scenes and others lasting shorter with fewer scenes, depending on the genre and the needs of the story and characters. The length of *Act 1* is about *one-fourth* (occasionally a bit shorter) of the overall story; *Act 2* is about the *middle* half, quarters two (2A) and three (2B); *Act 3* is about the *last fourth* (occasionally a bit shorter). Using a 100-page screenplay as an example, Act 1 is about pages 1–25; Act 2A is about pages 26–50; Act 2B is about pages 50–75; Act 3 is about pages 76 to 100. As script buyers call for shorter scripts, you might consider an 80-page script: Act 1 = pages 1–20; Act 2A = pages 21–40; Act 2B = pages 41–60; Act 3 = pages 61–80.

Reflection and Discussion

1. It is said that everyone has at least one good story idea. What is yours? If you have more than one, select one. Considering the elements of plot discussed in this chapter, outline the plot of your best story idea. Be sure to divide the plot into fourths and follow the three-act structure. Be careful of **deus ex machina**, or a contrived plot device that appears out of nowhere to get the story moving (named after the "machine of the god" used in some ancient greek plays that would lower a god or goddess from above the stage or "out of the blue" to resolve a problem.) Characters, objects, events, or skills should arise organically from the story to move it along.
2. Think of your favorite film, or pick one favorite if you have more than one. Chances are that one of the reasons you like this film is because the story engaged you from beginning to end. Chances are also that the film follows the three-act

structure. Identify the scene that serves as the inciting incident. Next, locate the unforeseen surprise crisis that ends Act 1 and launches the hero or heroine into the journey that begins Act 2A (about one-fourth of the way in). Now, find the midpoint ordeal that the protagonist overcomes that ends Act 2A and results in a moment of reward that begins Act 2B (about half-way). Move along through the hero's fall until his or her lowest possible point that ends Act 2B, followed by the spark that turns things around and gets him or her going again at the start of Act 3 (about three-fourths of the way). Finally, describe the climax, when the protagonist defeats the antagonist, and the denouement that follows with a glimpse of how the protagonist and his or her world have changed.

3. Have you ever watched a film that was categorized as "experimental"? If not, see if you can find one online or in a library. Once you have watched one, how did the filmmaker experiment with plot that was different from the structure described here?

3

Character

Character is the second of Aristotle's elements. Translations from the Greek *ethos* also include "argument," "ego," "ethics," "intentions," and "manners." Character is the presentation of people by the actors. It is "who the play is about." The characters inhabit the conflicts that drive the dramatic plots (perhaps that's why this is the second longest chapter after "plot").

Character is often analyzed in terms of protagonists (a.k.a., heroes, good guys, white hats), antagonists (a.k.a., villains, bad guys, black hats), other principals who have major roles in the main plot ("A" story), supporting characters who have essential but lesser roles (a.k.a., those in the "B" stories or subplots), and functionaries (e.g., mentors, foils, messengers, confidants, raisonneurs, sidekicks, others who serve a function to move the story forward). Character is crucial in holding viewer interest. Our sympathies, or empathies, lie with the protagonist as he or she fights the antagonist.

Protagonists

Every story is one person's story. That person is the main character, or **protagonist**, sometimes called the hero, the good guy, the white hat (based on Westerns in which the good guy wore a white hat), and so on. In many cases, the protagonist is easy to spot. He or she might be the title character (e.g., *Jerry Maguire*, Crow 1996), or might have the most screen time (e.g., any Charlie Chaplin film), or might clearly drive the story (any Clint Eastwood film). Sometimes, though, there might seem to be two protagonists, as in the case of any love story (e.g., *An Affair to Remember*, McCarey 1957) or buddy-buddy story (e.g., *Rain Man*, Levison 1988). Sometimes more characters might appear to be protagonists, as in an **ensemble** script (e.g., *The Hangover*, Phillips 2009). In these cases, though, there is still a single protagonist. The other characters are major supporting characters or principal characters.

How does one determine the protagonist when it seems different characters compete for that position? The answer is the character who undergoes the biggest change, or arc (more anon). While all the major characters have arcs, the character with the principal arc is the main character. It is this arc, or change, that points to the theme (see Chapter 4). That is, the major lesson of the story is the same lesson that the major character learns; conversely whoever learns the story's theme is the protagonist. Additionally, protagonists are the ones who principally drive the story. While other characters make decisions that move the plot, the protagonist is the main person whose decisions, and reactions to others' decisions, embody the A-story.

Any romance film (comedy or drama) or buddy-buddy film (male or female buddies) illustrates this. Both lead characters go on the journey; both change as a result; both learn; both grow; both are necessary for the final resolution of the problem that drives the story. At first glance, then, it seems that both are protagonists. Upon deeper analysis, however, one of the two has to undergo a greater change than the other for the final climactic scene to happen. That is, one of the two leads starts the film farther away from the end—psychologically, emotionally, spiritually, and/or physically—so that character has farther to travel—literally and/or figuratively—to the final resolution.

The other lead character begins the story at least slightly closer to the finish and is functionally a major supporting character to the protagonist. Let's consider *Thelma and Louise* (Scott 1991). This is a much-heralded, female, buddy-buddy, road-trip film. Actually, many buddy-buddy films are also road-trip films, such as *Butch Cassidy and the Sundance Kid* (Hill 1969), which inspired *Thelma and Louise*. Thelma (Geena Davis) and Louise (Susan Sarandon) both hit the road to get away from bad relationships, are hunted by police, and end up driving off a cliff together. So whose story it is? Meek and mild Thelma is married to an abusive husband. She leaves him and her waitressing job to hit the road with Louise. Strong-headed, independent Louise is not married but is in a problematic relationship with a musician. Once on the road, Thelma wants to stop for a drink, where she is nearly raped by a man before Louise kills him. Now they are wanted for murder and head to Mexico. Along the way, Thelma picks up a hitchhiker (Brad Pitt), eventually making love to him and leaving him in her room with all the money the women have, which he steals. Among the many other story points, Louise refuses to go to Mexico by way of Texas—it seems she was raped there.

Based on these clues, which of the two undergoes the biggest change with the climactic decision to hold hands and drive the Thunderbird off the cliff? The answer is Thelma (Davis). She is timid, married, and has a job. In contrast, Louise is decisive, not married, and we don't know if she has a job. Thelma has to change more than Louise during the course of the story arcing from her timid life to a suicide pact. Thelma has to leave a husband and employment and learn to take charge. Louise has no husband and apparently no employment (or insignificant employment) and already knows how to take charge. So while both learn and grow through their adventure, Thelma has the principal arc. Additionally, it is her decisions that primarily drive the story, including stopping at the bar and later picking up the hitchhiker. She also holds up a gas station, stuffs a police officer in his car trunk, and other non-Thelma like behaviors as she arcs along the way. To be sure, Louise also makes decisions that are important to the story, such as killing Thelma's would-be rapist and leaving Thelma alone with the hitchhiker while she talks with her boyfriend. Still, it is Thelma's decisions, along with her reactions to Louise's decisions, that propel the story, right up to her final coaxing Louise to "keep going" over the cliff, even though Louise at first suggests surrender. This is Thelma's story.

Extraordinary Person in Ordinary Situation

Protagonists are either special people or common people. If they are special, the story comes from their facing common situations. For example, in *Superman* (Donner 1978), the hero of the same name (Christopher Reeve) is special. Given his super powers, we expect to see him in special situations, and we do, such as outrunning a train, saving a crashing helicopter, reversing the revolution of the earth, and the like. The audience needs to see his super powers in action for there to be a payoff. However, the story progresses through scenes in which Superman faces normal occurrences, such as trying to get the attention of the girl, Lois Lane (Margot Kidder). In these scenes, the extraordinary "super man" even has an ordinary name: Clark Kent. In watching this super person face the everyday, we learn his character traits, which in turn move the plot forward. This first category of protagonist may be stated as *an extraordinary person in an ordinary situation*.

Ordinary Person in Extraordinary Situation

In the case of a common-person protagonist, the opposite occurs: as the ordinary person faces the extraordinary, his or her character traits are revealed and that character drives the plot. Thelma in the above example of *Thelma and Louise* falls in this category. Another example is any *Die Hard* film. John McClane (Bruce Willis) is a somewhat average person with an average name. However, circumstance leads him to be a hero by defeating terrorists. If this normal guy only did normal things for two hours, like brush his teeth and drive to the store, there would be no story. It is in his rise to the very atypical situation into which he is thrust that makes the character and the story. In *La Llorona*, Guadalupe falls into this second category of protagonist: *an ordinary person in an extraordinary situation*. She is a common villager, but circumstance leads her to the horrific act of infanticide and its eternal consequence.

Achilles' Heel

Protagonists have a **character deficit** at the beginning of the story: something they must overcome or gain in order to resolve the conflict in the climax at the end of Act 3. This weakness is sometimes called an **Achilles' heel**, after the ancient Greek mythological hero Achilles who was held by his heel and dipped into the River Styx as a boy to make him invulnerable, but because his heel was not touched by the water it was left vulnerable, leading to his death as a young soldier when a poison arrow pierced his heel. The Achilles' heel, or weakness, might be a physical deficit as it was for Achilles. Superman is weakened when exposed to Kryptonite. Forrest Gump in the film of the same name (Zemeckis 1994) has braces on his legs as a boy, but he loses them to become a great runner—a skill that benefits him later. John Ferguson (James Steward) in *Vertigo* (Hitchcock 1958) must overcome a fear of heights. The character deficit might be an emotional or personality quirk: Marlin the Clown Fish in *Finding Nemo* (Stanton and Unkrich 2003) is afraid to leave the coral reef, but he must do so to save his son. In an example from a popular television series, psychiatrist Frasier Crane (*Frasier*, 1993–2004) must overcome a fear of clowns in one episode before he can properly tend to his father—a most interesting Achilles' heel for a psychiatrist whose profession involves helping others overcome their fears. The weakness might also be a physical object that is required to accomplish an objective: Dorothy in *The Wizard of Oz* (Fleming 1939) needs ruby slippers to assist her on her journey. Luke Skywalker in *Star Wars* (Lucas 1977) needs a light saber to do battle.

Arc

The protagonist's progression is called an **arc**: the change the hero experiences. He or she is a different person at the end of the story than at the beginning. He or she has learned something about himself or herself, and about life, as a consequence of going on the journey. All the obstacles and conflicts and confrontations and trials and tribulations and training and meeting mentors and allies and enemies move the protagonist along the arc as he or she learns something from each unsuccessful attempt to resolve the major conflict. There might be momentary successes along the way, most notably at the midpoint. In fact, overcoming the midpoint ordeal foreshows the ending climax—the final resolution of the conflict (see Chapter 2). However, while the protagonist learns enough in the first half of the story to have a moment of triumph at the midpoint, he or she is only half-way through his or her arc at that midpoint, so the Achilles' heel resurfaces soon in the second half, leading to the hero's lowest point at the end of Act 2 (see Chapter 2). The hero then experiences the spark back to life (beginning of Act 3—see Chapter 2), and—after a few more obstacles that provide the final challenges—the protagonist has learned and mastered all that is necessary to arrive at the climactic scene. Because of his or her arc—the lessons learned—he or she is finally victorious in vanquishing the antagonist.

The major lesson the protagonist learns is the story's theme (see Chapter 4). Without learning that lesson, the hero cannot finish the job he or she set out to do in the beginning. In learning that theme, the protagonist completes his or her arc and can engage in the story's climax. For example, in *Gone with the Wind* (Fleming 1939), Scarlett O'Hara (Vivien Leigh) undergoes epic trials in the course of her journey, from multiple husbands to the Civil War to her father losing his mind to the death of her child, all of which give her the resolve she needs in the end to state that she will go home ("return to Tara") when her last husband, Rhett Butler (Clark Gable), walks out on her. In *The Wizard of Oz* (Fleming 1939), Dorothy (Judy Garland) goes on a wonderfully colorful and spectacular fantasy adventure with the overarching need to get back home. She is not able to achieve that goal and conclude her journey until she learns that "there's no place like home." With the completion of that arc—lesson learned—she can finally return to her Kansas farm (with some help from an ally, the Good Witch Glinda, of course).

The Wizard of Oz also provides an example of how other characters arc, as well, though again the biggest arc belongs to the protagonist. The Scarecrow, the Tin Man, and the Lion all have Achilles' heels (no brain, no heart, and no courage, respectively). However, each demonstrates that he actually does possess this quality within. For example, as the three hunker down outside the evil castle, the Scarecrow comes up with a plan (thought in his brain), while the Tin Man weeps for sorrow at Dorothy being trapped inside (feeling in his heart), and the Lion declares that he's ready to go face the impending danger for Dorothy (courageous action in his soul). Ultimately, the Wizard confirms that each has possessed his supposedly missing trait all along, and he bestows upon each a gift that represents that quality (honorary diploma, heart on a chain, and medal of valor, respectively). Their arcs reinforce Dorothy's major arc as she learns from Glinda in the climactic moment that she has possessed the ability to return home all along; she merely had to learn that for herself. She states the film's theme, clicks her heels three times, completes her journey, and returns home for the denouement.

Sometimes, the protagonist's arc is not so much a change as it is a reaffirmation of what is right. For example, in *To Kill a Mockingbird* (Mulligan 1962), attorney Atticus Finch (Gregory Peck) starts and ends as an upright and just man. His arc is a reaffirmation of his belief that all people deserve equal treatment, regardless of race. In the

James Bond franchise, Bond remains loyal to the Queen throughout, risking life and limb to thwart global terrorists for the sake of country (England). Other examples include *Gladiator* (Scott 2000) and *Lincoln* (Spielberg 2012), both of which feature protagonists who hold to what is good and right: Maximus battling the evil Emperor Commodus (Joaquin Phoenix) for the sake of country (Rome) and Lincoln fighting for the 13th Constitutional Amendment to abolish slavery for the sake of country (America). Even though these protagonists do not change, but rather reaffirm, their moral stances, they are different at the ends of the stories than they were at the beginnings. They are changed because of their sticking to what is right, whether they end up dead (Maximus, Lincoln) or alive (Finch, Bond).

In the case of *La Llorona*, Guadalupe undergoes change. She arcs from unwed mother to banished villager to murderess to lost soul. She learns that actions have consequences, and the consequence she must accept for having illegitimate children, killing them, and losing their bodies, is an eternity of wandering the earth, crying and moaning as the mournful wind called *La Llorona*. One can argue that the supporting character of the child in the framing story also undergoes a secondary arc. He or she cannot sleep at the start of the story because of the mournful wind; however, at the end, the child is able to sleep, having decided that Guadalupe's guilt has finally ended—she has found her babies as the wind dies down.

Antagonists

The character who stands in the way of the protagonist achieving his or her overall objective to the greatest extent is the **antagonist**, sometimes called the villain, the bad guy, the black hat, and so on. There might be more than one character who throws obstacles in the way of the protagonist (e.g., the various sea creatures in *Finding Nemo*), but the one who causes the most difficulty and the last one to be defeated in the end is the antagonist (e.g., humans, the ultimate bad guys, in *Finding Nemo*). Antagonists are usually one or more of three types: *another character,* an *external force*—such as the environment, circumstance, fate, god/s—or an *internal force* within the protagonist him or herself—the Achilles' heel that he or she must overcome. Some theorists make this point by stating the three kinds of conflict between protagonist and antagonist this way: *human v. human, human v. nature, human v. self.* In many cases, the antagonist might be two or all three types.

Human v. Human

The human antagonist is the personification of the protagonist's weakness. That is, the antagonist is the flip side, or dark side, of the protagonist. The antagonist has the protagonist's Achilles' heel, but he or she has it "in spades." The antagonist is the protagonist run wild, unleashed and unchecked. He or she is what the protagonist would become if the protagonist did not have—or find during the course of the story—a moral center that keeps him or her from spiraling out of control. This serves a story's structure well because the protagonist must face his or her own weakness in facing the antagonist. The hero sees his or her own demon in the villain and must first overcome that demon in himself or herself to defeat the bad guy in the climactic scene.

For example, in the *Batman* franchise of films (Warner Bros.), each bad guy embodies some characteristic of the haunted Batman, but the bad guy has succumbed to psychosis in his or her lust for revenge, while the Batman struggles to keep his inner dark side in check while fighting for the good of Gotham City. In Steven Spielberg's *Schindler's List* (1993), Oskar Schindler (Liam Neeson) is an industrialist and an opportunist, taking advantage of the Nazis rounding up Jews to use those Jews as free labor in his factories, thereby increasing his profit margin as he sells his goods to those same Nazis who supply him with Jews. He faces this Achilles' heel of amoral opportunism in the personification of Amon Goeth (Ralph Fiennes). Goeth has no moral compass; he passes time as an unchecked opportunist, seeking the pleasure of women and alcohol, sometimes killing a Jew in anger or just for fun as target practice. If Schindler did not eventually find his moral center, realizing that he has the power and ultimately the obligation to save Jewish lives, he could become another Nazi like Goeth, moping about, trying to find meaning in physical pleasure and moral decay.

In *Finding Nemo*, humans are the ultimate antagonists, first the dentist who captures Nemo and later the fishermen in the film's climax. It is humanity's lust to control its environment that leads humanity to serve as the principal antagonist of this story, more than the secondary antagonists of the sharks, jellyfish, seagulls, and so on. Marlin, the protagonist, also seeks to control his environment by keeping his son Nemo at home, safely on the coral reef. He also tries to keep control by attempting to talk Dory out of going with the sharks or talking with the whale. Yet, it is Dory's fearless sense of adventure (the opposite of Marlin), combined with her short-term memory loss, that leads Marlin to follow this ally, ultimately finding his son. In doing so, he arcs by learning to "let go" of his son (theme) so that his son can live his own life. If only those antagonistic humans would let go of their need for control and learn to "live and let live."

Human v. Environment

The environment in which the protagonist finds himself or herself also serves as a type of antagonist. Continuing with the same three examples, Gotham City—with its fear and oppression and darkness—is the environmental antagonist of the *Batman* films. That fearful, oppressive, and dark world is caused by the human antagonist of each film (Joker, etc.), so the environment serves as an extension of that same dark evil that the human antagonist represents, and that the protagonist must overcome within himself. In *Schindler's List*, Nazi Germany is the enemy environment. Schindler grew up in a Germany of a different time and must adapt to Nazi rule to continue to make his fortune. In adapting, however, he almost loses his soul, as has happened with the person antagonist, Goeth. Schindler, however, comes to realize from the Jews under his care, particularly his bookkeeper Itzhak Stern (Ben Kingsley) who types the names of prisoners that Schindler wants working for him on a list, that his "list is life." He is called to overcome the evil environment and save his fellow humans. In *Finding Nemo*, the open ocean serves as the environmental antagonist. It represents the fear Marlin has of ever leaving the safety of his own home, the Great Barrier Reef. In addition to being home to other antagonistic creatures, such as sharks who are trying to break their fish-eating habit, a scary whale who turns out to be an ally, and so on, the ocean also leads to land where that ultimate antagonist resides—humans. Marlin must face this wide open ocean environment to overcome his own inability to let go of his son.

Human v. Self

This third type of antagonist—the protagonist's own self in his or her weakness, or internal character deficit—has already been discussed in the previous sections. Batman's haunted past at having witnessed the murder of his parents leads him to face down the psychotic bad guys and gals who have succumbed to revenge lust because of their own haunted pasts. Schindler must overcome his own desire for immediate gratification and wealth to save Jewish lives rather than end up like Goeth. Marlin must overcome his fear of the unknown ocean and the ultimate enemy, humans, to learn to stop being overprotective of his son and let him go to make his own mistakes, have his own journeys, and ultimately live his own life.

All three types of antagonists—human, environment, and self—are found in many screenplays. Our sample script, *La Llorona*, illustrates this. The *human* antagonists are Guadalupe's fellow villagers, exemplified by the old hag who serves as the primary antagonist. She is the one who announces the birth of the bastard twins, while the villagers react with shame and shunning. The *environmental* conflict consists of the social and religious norms of the time. The villagers embody the notion that this woman and her children are unholy, and this leads to the oppressive and frightening society that Guadalupe must face. Her *internal conflict* is Guadalupe's own guilt and shame, first at having babies out of wedlock, second at killing them, and third at losing their bodies in the river. Notice how the villagers have this same characteristic of guilt and shame, but without a check on them. All are guilty of their own sins because all are human (perhaps some even had sex before marriage or even gave birth secretly to illegitimate children); yet, they mill about expressing hypocritical shock and disgust at Guadalupe's having children outside of wedlock.

Instead of attempting to resolve her own guilt through feigned piety, as the villagers do, Guadalupe chooses a different option. She finds the resolve to do the unthinkable: kill her own children. As horrific as this act is, it demonstrates an inner strength. It is possible the villagers will brandish torches one night and storm her hut to take her babies and kill them, anyway, so if her twins are going to die, she is resolved to be the one who kills them. Of course, her infanticide does not alleviate her guilt, but only multiplies it. She does not walk back to the village after doing the deed, announcing that her children are dead so life can return to normal. Instead, the greatest of all possible guilt overwhelms her—the guilt of murdering her own children. She frantically attempts to find their drowned bodies so she can at least give them a proper burial, but to no avail. Her fate is sealed. Unlike the antagonistic villagers and the shunning environment they create, she overcomes her own inner guilt and shame by succumbing to her destiny: wandering the earth, weeping like a sad wind, trying to find her babies so she can lay them to rest, along with her own soul.

Supporting Characters

In addition to the protagonists and antagonists, stories have **supporting characters**. These are the major secondary characters who round out the A-, B-, and C-stories. They are not the leads, but they receive enough screen time to develop their characteristics more than functionaries (next subsection). Supporting characters complement the protagonist and antagonist, often serving as their opposite types. This is necessary to thrust the protagonists into action—someone has to make them overcome the Achilles' heel that would otherwise keep them from going on the journey. Often, supporting characters serve a **mentor** role, or a **confidant**, or a **raisonneur**, giving advice and sometimes physical gifts to help the protagonists just when they need help (e.g., Obi-Wan Kenobi's gift of a light saber to Luke Skywalker in *Star Wars*). Supporting characters might also be enemies instead of allies, in which case their role complements the antagonist rather than the protagonist. They round out the negative forces the hero must face (e.g., the sharks and jellyfish in *Finding Nemo*). Supporting characters have their own weaknesses (Obi-Wan is old compared to Luke's youth; the sharks are trying to overcome their fish addiction), but they complement the protagonist by filling in the void caused by his or her deficits, or they complement the antagonist by filling in some trait that he or she is missing.

Some previous examples illustrate further. In *Thelma and Louise*, timid Thelma would not leave her husband and job were it not for her opposite friend, decisive Louise. Outgoing capitalist Schindler would not learn to oppose Nazi tyranny against the Jews unless his opposite, thoughtful bookkeeper Stern, guided his moral compass to compassion. Agoraphobic and pessimistic Marlin would not venture all the way from his coral reef into Sydney Harbor were it not for his opposite, happy-go-lucky Dory, who optimistically leads the way.

Supporting characters also fill in the secondary and tertiary stories: the B- and C-stories. In some cases, they are part of the protagonist's story from the beginning, but they have their own parallel stories, too. For example, both Marlin and Nemo are together in the beginning, but after Nemo's capture by the scuba-diving dentist, Nemo's B-story separates from his father's A-story, though they are parallel. As Marlin ventures through the ocean, Nemo experiences parallel adventures in the fish tank. Marlin finds himself away from home with a strange blue fish; Nemo finds himself in a tank with strange fish. Marlin almost dies in a jellyfish encounter; Nemo almost dies trying to jam the tank's filter system. Marlin has a breakthrough when a friendly whale spews Dory and him from its blowhole into Sydney Harbor; Nemo has a breakthrough when he finally jams the fan. Of course, the A- and B-stories must come together by the end for a satisfying story, unified in theme (see Chapter 8). This happens in Act 3 when Marlin and Nemo reunite in the fishing grounds for their final, climactic trial. Likewise in a second example, Forrest Gump and Jenny meet as schoolchildren; their lives go separate ways with occasional crossings; and finally they are united again in marriage, though Jenny soon succumbs to AIDS.

In other cases, B-story characters might not know each other at the beginning; nevertheless, they live parallel lives unbeknownst to each other, but their lives are thematically united. Ultimately, their paths cross: the A- and B-stories (and C- and any other stories) come together. *Crash* (Haggis 2004) serves as an example. In this ensemble film, the Los Angeles' characters live different lives infected by racism (the unifying theme, see Chapter 4), but eventually the audience sees the connection among the divergent stories when they converge.

Functionaries

Beyond protagonists, antagonists, and major supporting characters, a story needs occasional **functionaries**. These are the other characters who appear briefly as needed for the story. They do not get much screen time, perhaps just one line or a few lines in a single scene, so they do not develop much. If they have no lines, unless they are a muted supporting character or a mime, they are background actors, formerly known as extras. Background actors have their function, as well: filling in a scene, such as people in a restaurant.

Functionaries do whatever the story needs at the moment it needs it. Vogler (2007) lists some mythological functionary types. He notes the hero and mentor, but also lists other character types who might be developed to the point of supporting characters or might appear just once to perform the functions that their names imply: threshold guardian, herald, shapeshifter, shadow, ally, and trickster. In the best scripts, these functionaries appear organically at the time and place the story needs them, rather than appearing for no reason other than to make a point. For example, in *The Wizard of Oz* (Fleming 1939), the singing Munchkins—who live in Munchkinland where Dorothy has landed—send Dorothy down the yellow brick road in song. In a personal favorite of mine, *Raising Arizona* (Coen brothers 1987), two bank robbers are confused by an elderly bank customer when they give the conflicting orders to the people in the bank, "Everybody freeze," followed by, "Everybody down on the ground." The functionary old hayseed replies, "Well, which is it, young feller? You want l should freeze or get down on the ground? I mean to say, if I freeze, I can't rightly drop, and if I drop, I'm gonna be in motion. You see?" In *Titanic* (Cameron 1997), after Rose (Kate Winslet) contemplates jumping from the ship and is talked down by Jack (Leonardo DiCaprio), a haughty British aristocrat suggests that the wealthy gents return to their brandy and cigars, serving the function of showing the callousness of the upper crust—class distinctions being central to the story.

Unmasking

The protagonist's adventure from the setup to the resolution of the conflict results in an **unmasking** of the character. As with the arc, other characters, including the antagonist, are also unmasked, but the protagonist undergoes the greatest unmasking. At the open of any story, we know nothing about this person: he or she is masked. By the end, we know what is necessary about this person for the story: he or she is unmasked. At different steps, or **beats**, along the way, different character attributes are uncovered. Some use the metaphor of **peeling an onion**, revealing one layer at a time. Through the action in which each character engages, and through the dialogue, if any, he or she speaks (with literal meaning or some other subtext—see Chapter 5), the character's **back story** is revealed, unmasking who this person is. For example, in Clint Eastwood's classic "Spaghetti Western" films, his character is introduced as a loner who rides into town. We know nothing about him at first, but as the story unfolds, we learn of the abuse he endured in the past, ultimately realizing that this hardened man has returned to right that wrong.

In *La Llorona*, we know nothing about Guadalupe at the beginning other than that she gives birth to illegitimate twins. Then we see her determination as she walks through the village gantlet. Next, we see how that strong will culminates in cruelty as she drowns her children. If the story ended at that midpoint, she would be merely heartless. But she has a heart. We see that in her realization of the horror of what she has done and her flailing attempt to recover the bodies. Her remorse reveals her conscience. We learn that she loved her children: she constructs a makeshift grave for them. Her compassion, grief, and guilt come to a head in the sealing of her fate, the climax at which she is fully unmasked: her soul must continue its search for peace.

Ethos, Pathos, and Hybris

For the viewers to be drawn into a character's struggle and change, that character must in some way relate. The audience must be able to identify with something in the hero, to feel **sympathy** for him or her, if not **empathy**. It is the progression of this sympathetic protagonist that endears him or her to the viewers and holds their interest.

The writer creates sympathy and empathy by unmasking ethos and pathos in the characters. **Ethos**, the word that Aristotle uses for "character" and the word from which "ethical" comes, refers to the moral standards of a character, and more broadly to his or her attitudes and habits. These character traits are revealed in the protagonist's dilemma: to run away from the leading conflict or to overcome seemingly impossible obstacles to resolve it? The hero first attempts to avoid the driving conflict of the story (refuses the call, see Chapter 2), but for the story to unfold as drama, the hero must eventually fight—physically, intellectually, emotionally, spiritually, or some combination of these. The total package of traits that leads the protagonist to his or her decisions in this fight—this road to resolution—are the ethos that draws us to this character.

In *La Llorona*, Guadalupe's shame of illegitimate children leads her to kill them, and her love for her children leads her to remorse for her action. Her guilt temporarily supersedes her compassion as she pushes aside her moral conscience to drown her babies, hoping falsely that this immoral act will ease the burden of guilt. Of course it does not. Instead, the guilt intensifies as the shame of illegitimate children gives way to remorse for committing infanticide. The consequence of her choices is that Guadalupe's soul cannot find rest but must roam forever in a supernatural quest to find her babies and bury them rightfully. These twins, born into and killed in their mother's sin, must be laid to proper rest before the mother can be laid to rest. This package of character traits constitute Guadalupe's ethos, which draws us to her character.

Pathos, from which the word "pathetic" comes, refers to that quality in the protagonist that makes him or her worthy of the audience's pity. This notion stems originally from tragedy, in which the protagonist is brought down in the end, though he or she still resolves the conflict. In the struggles that make up the story that eventually leads to his or her end, the audience feels pity. This quality is also found in the protagonists of comedy, melodrama, and other forms of story. If the viewers do not have any feeling for the protagonist, they will not engage in the story. The writer must unmask the pathos of the protagonist to draw in the viewers. We must grow to care about this character as we learn more about him or her. If we do not care, the drama is lost on us. The protagonist's pathos arouses our sympathy for his or her journey.

In *La Llorona*, we are drawn to Guadalupe's story because circumstance has led her to make very hard choices, just as our lives call us to make difficult choices. The consequences of her actions are as difficult as the actions themselves, just as the consequences of some of our actions are. Our choices and consequences hopefully are not the same as Guadalupe's: I sincerely hope no readers ever feel compelled to hurt or kill their children and experience the doom of everlasting guilt. Still, our understanding of the notion of difficult choices and their consequences arouses pity for Guadalupe. We feel for her as she reveals a depth of human character in her emotions and actions. This determined, compassionate woman is brought by circumstances—both external and internal—to commit a deed so terrible that it leads to her eternal grief, remorse, and punishment. She experiences a full range of human qualities: shame, love, compassion, social entrapment, the need for atonement for wrongdoing, remorse, guilt, sorrow, and ever-elusive redemption. A character this richly textured demonstrates pathos. These human qualities make us care about what happens to her.

Another character concept that is unmasked, or revealed, as the story progresses is **hybris**, alternate spelling **hubris**, referring to the protagonist's boastful or arrogant pride. This is not rightful pride at a job well done, but rather an excess of pride that prevents appropriate humility. It is often this pride that ultimately leads the protagonist to his or her journey, but in the end brings him or her to ruin in tragedy or to his or her comeuppance in comedy. This concept also stems from the writings of Aristotle about tragedy specifically, but it applies to comedy, melodrama, and other forms, as well. While the hero is not ruined in comedy or melodrama, it is still often his or her pride that provides stumbling blocks and complications along the way to the final resolution of the problem.

An example from tragedy illustrates hybris. Sophocles' *Oedipus the King* (*c.* 429 BCE) (see Chapter 5, Figure 5.1) is the seminal poetic drama on which Aristotle based his ideas. In this classic play, the title character declares punishment on the person responsible for angering the gods and bringing a plague upon Thebes. He suspects his brother-in-law, Creon—the human antagonist. Later, Oedipus learns that he is himself the culprit, having unknowingly fulfilled a prophecy from his birth that he would one day murder his father and marry his mother. To resolve his external conflict—his predetermined destiny—a prophecy from the gods—fate, he must confront an internal conflict—his own hybris. Ultimately, he blinds himself and banishes himself from Thebes, carrying out his own punishment. Other writers offer additional analyses of character, including ethos, pathos, hybris, and other useful concepts (e.g., Egri 1946; Nicoll 1931; Seger 2010; Stanislavski 1936).

Experiments with Character

As with plot, some dramatists experiment with the traditional concept of character, creating people who alienate, rather than reach, the viewers. In unmasking their characters, these writers purposely attempt to reveal character traits that do not elicit pathos from the audience, but instead elicit critical reflection. For example, the iconoclastic Bertolt Brecht (1898–1956) developed a theory of "epic theater" in which he believed the viewers should not be emotionally engaged with the characters, leading to catharsis (see Chapter 9), but instead should engage in their own thoughtful analysis of the staged play to recognize society's injustices, leading to social change. In his plays (e.g., *The Threepenny Opera* 1928; *Mother Courage and Her Children* 1939), he never allows the audience to become sympathetic toward the characters. He constantly reminds the viewers of the artificiality of the stage. The characters are not real people; they are merely portrayals of types.

While Brecht's experimentation with non-sympathetic characters reveals his genius, it also makes the point that conventional characters endear themselves to the audience as they fight to resolve the conflict with the antagonist. Brecht is something of an exception that proves the rule. Because his characters are rarely endearing, his stories usually attract smaller audiences (though very attentive ones) than stories with characters who demonstrate greater universal appeal (which was just fine with the iconoclastic Brecht).

In film, this Brechtian tradition can be seen not only in filmed versions of his plays but in some semi-popular works, as well. Two examples come to mind: *Gangs of New York* (Scorsese 2002) and *There Will Be Blood* (Anderson 2007). In these films, both starring Daniel Day-Lewis, the protagonist demonstrates no real endearing qualities, leading to alienation rather than sympathy from the audience. Viewers are left to think about the injustice of the immoral, bullying, and murderous protagonist rather than feel enduring sympathy for him. Again, as with Brecht, these films are exceptions to the rule that writers traditionally unmask protagonists by revealing enduring, if flawed, qualities to engage viewers emotionally. By the way, lest any readers mistakenly think that Day-Lewis plays only non-sympathetic characters, he also plays the very sympathetic Abraham Lincoln in *Lincoln* (Spielberg 2012), as well as a host of other traditionally sympathetic protagonists (e.g., *My Left Foot*, Sheridan 1989; *The Last of the Mohicans*, Mann 1992).

Character Types

An understanding of different types of characters is important to successful story writing. The subject of character types and personality traits has been part of human study through the millennia. Here are some examples of personality typologies that are useful in creating characters' personalities. These typologies are simplified overviews of different scholars' work. For a fuller understanding of each, please read the cited texts.

Four humors

Ancient literature, attributed first to Hippocrates (c. 460–370 BCE) and later to Galen (ACE 130–201), includes discussions of four personality types based on the dominance of one of four bodily fluids, or humors (see Figure 3.1). To be in "good humor" the fluids were said to be in correct balance or harmony. **Sanguine**: an abundance of blood was associated with happiness and passion—a pounding heart makes one strong and confident. **Phlegmatic**: too much phlegm, or mucus, led one to be apathetic and dull—the flu with its runny nose and cough makes you want to lie down and sleep. **Melancholic**: too much black bile backed up in the digestive system caused sadness and depression (melancholy)—constipation can bring a person down,

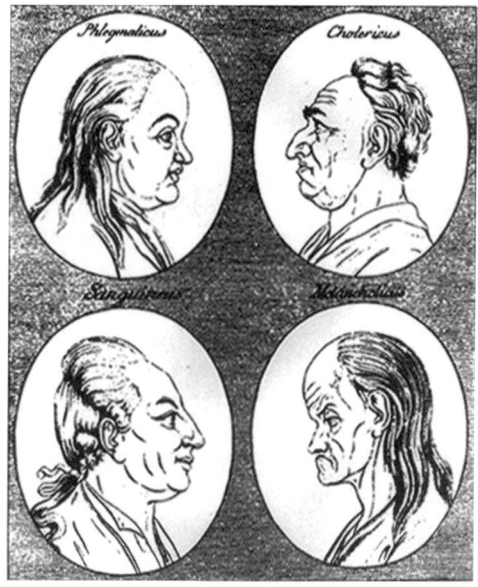

Figure 3.1 The four humors, an early categorization of personality types: clockwise from top left—phlegmatic, choleric, melancholic, sanguine

but oh how the spirit lifts when the dark feces is discharged (physicians would sometimes give depressed patients a laxative). **Choleric**: an abundance of yellow bile, or urine, was responsible for anger and ill humor—everyone gets irritable when they have to "go" (physicians would sometimes give angry, feverish patients a diuretic—perhaps leading to the phrase "pissed off").

Enneagram

Riso and Hudson (1996) explore the ancient **Enneagram**. This "nine-point diagram" (*ennea* is Greek for nine) is a useful study of personality types (see Figure 3.2). The types are clustered into three broad triads of three personalities each. The "Feeling Triad" consists of the "Helper," "Motivator," and "Individualist." The "Thinking Triad"

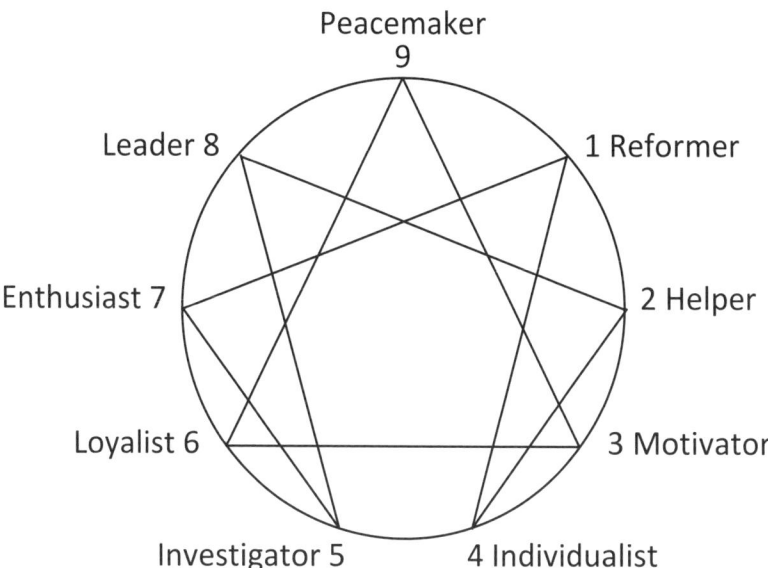

Figure 3.2 The Enneagram typology of personality, according to Riso and Hudson

is made up of the "Investigator," "Loyalist," and "Enthusiast." The "Relating Triad," also called the "Instinctive Triad," is comprised of the "Leader," "Peacemaker," and "Reformer." Each point has two lines that lead to two other points, making other triads of types. These types are broad brushstrokes of personalities. They point to dominant or overall traits, understanding that no one is wholly one type (one-dimensional), but everyone possesses many character traits (multi-dimensional). The placement of adjacent types on the diagram is significant: each personality has some characteristic traits of the adjacent personalities. Additionally, each type is best complemented by an opposite type across the circle.

Sigmund Freud (1856–1939)

Psychologists have long studied character traits. For example, Freud (1917) argued that personalities develop from either oral, anal, or phallic fixations. He modified these with a second dimension of a person's tendencies: receptive, retentive, or expulsive. He also developed the constructs of the id, ego, and superego (1923). These three dimensions of Freud's work may be diagrammed into a model (see Figure 3.3). This model can be useful in placing dramatic characters at different points in the scheme, developing their traits, and placing different types either in opposition to each other or in complementary positions to each other.

Carl Jung (1875–1961)

Jung (1921) presented "psychological types" along eight personality categories. He began with two opposites types along a continuum: extroversion and introversion. He crossed these with a second dimension consisting of four mental functions: feeling, thinking, sensation, and intuition. This yielded eight general types (see Figure 3.3). Again, this diagram can be useful in developing character traits along each dimension.

Figure 3.3 Carl Jung (1875–1961) and Sigmund Freud (1856–1939), two pioneers of psychology with summary models of their work on personality

Myers-Briggs

Myers and Briggs (myersbriggs.org) applied and expanded Jung's work in developing their well-known, 16-type, Myers-Briggs' Type Indicator (MBTI). This model maps psychological types along four dimensions with two polar types in each dimension:

- Extroversion (E) or Introversion (I)
- Sensing (S) or Intuition (N)
- Thinking (T) or Feeling (F)
- Judging (J) or Perceiving (P)

These four dimensions of two opposites each yield 16 possible combinations, or personality types ("ESTJ," "INFP," etc.). Each type is defined by a set of descriptors. This has become a useful tool in the industry for managers to build working teams with complementary people. It is also popular with script writers in developing their characters with certain dominant traits, rounded out with secondary traits.

Lajos Egri (1888–1967)

In addition to philosophers and psychologists, many dramatists also analyze character. One of the most-quoted dramatic theorists, Egri (1946), lays out traits along three dimensions, leading to **three-dimensional characters**: characters who demonstrate fully rounded attributes rather than single-minded, or superficial, one-dimensional qualities only.

- **Physiology**: sex, age, height and weight, color of hair, eyes and skin, posture, appearance, defects, and heredity.
- **Sociology**: class, occupation, education, home life, religion, race and nationality, place in community, political affiliations, and amusements or hobbies.
- **Psychology**: sex life and moral standards, personal premise or ambition, frustrations or chief disappointments, temperament (related to the four humors), attitude toward life, complexes, extrovert-introvert-ambivert, abilities, qualities, and IQ (pp. 36–37).

Armer (1993) expands on Egri, listing six character qualities: physical appearance, actions (or lack thereof), words, traits-mannerisms, effect on other characters, and names (p. 88). Dyas (1993) also reflects this typology, listing five character variables that dramatists manipulate: names, physical appearances, dialogue, behaviors, and personality traits (p. 100).

These are just some examples of the many psychological and dramatic analyses of character. The people who populate drama should be painted with the full color palette of personality traits and character idiosyncrasies. They should have dimension, and in that dimension they reach out to the audience. They pull us into their stories because we recognize something in them, some dimension that makes them fascinating to us.

Some additional examples illustrate. An aging man grows bitter, lying, and scornful as his career comes to an end; yet, he demonstrates tender, endearing, childish qualities (*Death of a Salesman*, Miller 1949). A man institutionalized for aggression seems normal compared with the other asylum inmates (*One Flew Over the Cuckoo's Nest*, Forman 1975). A young girl tries to get home after being blown away by a tornado, and along her journey she befriends a smart scarecrow with no brain (the last one you'd expect to come up with a plan to save her), a sensitive tin man with no heart (the last one you'd expect to weep when they lose her), and a fearless lion with no courage (the last one you'd expect to talk back to a frightening wizard) (you know this one—*The Wizard of Oz*, Fleming 1939).

Obsession

While all the characters should be drawn with a full array of interesting, consistent, and also idiosyncratic character traits that make them human, it is the protagonists whose characters we get to know fully. Whatever their personal qualities, these heroes and antiheroes always have something they want more than anything else. They have an **obsession** for which they will do anything: a **MacGuffin** for which they will engage in battle against the antagonist. This is their overarching **passion**. If they have no passion, they could simply walk away from the conflict, resulting in no story. For story, principal characters must go after their obsessions with everything they have, discovering some buried trait or talent they might not have even known they had, which leads them to resolution, one way or another.

For example, that most famous of all Shakespearean title characters, *Hamlet* (1603) (see Chapter 5, Figure 5.2), is sent by the ghost of his father on a quest to kill his stepfather, who is also his uncle and father's brother and murderer. But Hamlet is the thinking, brooding type ("To be or not to be?"), not given to action. His objective—to kill—conflicts with who he is—contemplator. In the climax, resolution occurs after he is pierced by a poison sword and learns of his uncle's treacherous plot to kill him. His blood boiling, he finally overcomes his contemplative nature and lunges into action, stabbing his uncle and forcing poisoned wine down his throat, just before he himself dies.

In the movies, we learn in the opening sequence of *Raiders of the Lost Ark* (Spielberg 1981) that Indiana Jones (Harrison Ford) is afraid of snakes, so naturally, to accomplish his goal—obtaining the lost Ark of the Covenant—he must encounter snakes again and overcome his fear. In *The Polar Express* (Zemeckis 2004), a young boy (Tom Hanks) takes the train ride of a lifetime, overcoming his doubts about Christmas and learning to believe again. In *The Godfather* (Coppola 1972), Michael Corleone (Al Pacino) wants to lead a legitimate life outside the family's mafia business, but his obsession to avenge his brother's murder overtakes his desire for legitimacy, and he is pulled back into the mob. On television, in *Downton Abbey* (2010–present), Robert Crawley (Hugh Bonneville) struggles to hold onto the old, aristocratic, British way of life, and to keep his castle, in the face of a changing 1920s' world.

In comedy, King Arthur (Graham Chapman) wants to find the Holy Grail, but too many silly diversions pop up (*Monty Python and the Holy Grail*, Gilliam and Jones 1975). In the popular television series *Seinfeld* (1990–1998), the four principal characters all want happiness and relationships, but their own narcissism leads them to settle for immediate gratification (e.g., sex, cigars, Chinese food, mocking others), leaving them self-centered and ultimately unfulfilled. You can think of your own examples of romantic comedies in which a boy or girl wants another girl or boy but cannot have him or her because they come from different families or live in different worlds (the original *Romeo and Juliet* story, Shakespeare 1597—though that's a tragedy).

Yet, the climactic scenes of romantic comedies find the couple happily in each other's arms, having overcome the obstacles to their love (unlike Romeo and Juliet who end up in each other's arms, but dead). The point is that characters have obsessions to achieve something. The stories happen as they encounter obstacle after obstacle to achieve that something. Along the way, layers of their personalities and their previous experiences are revealed: the traits and back story that have led them to where they are now. In those traits and life experiences, the viewers recognize something real, something to which they can relate. They can't wait to find out what happens next to these people in whom they have become emotionally invested. When the story ends, they feel satisfied because the characters have brought them through cathartic laughter and tears, with some surprises along the way.

Summary

Dramatic **characters** have been both created and studied for millennia. Every story features one **protagonist**: either an **extraordinary person in an ordinary situation** or an **ordinary person in an extraordinary situation**. These main characters have an **Achilles' heel** or inner deficit that they must overcome to complete their **arcs**, experiencing change and learning the moral lesson or **theme**, ultimately able to defeat the **antagonists**. Antagonists represent the protagonists' weaknesses, but exaggerated and unchecked. Antagonists might be characters, the environment, and/or the protagonist himself or herself, setting up three basic story types: **human v. human**, **human v. environment**, and/or **human v. self**. **Supporting** characters and **functionaries** round out the story. Major characters, principally the protagonist, are **unmasked** along the way as each **back story** is revealed piece by piece, as if **peeling an onion**. The dramatist reveals the characters' **ethos**, **pathos**, and **hybris** to arouse **sympathy** or **empathy** in the viewers, making them care about the heroes, flaws and all.

Philosophers, psychologists, and dramatists have studied characters' personalities for millennia, presenting different schemata of **personality types**. These include, among others, the **four humors**, the **Enneagram**, and the works of *Freud, Jung, Myers-Briggs*, and *Egri*. Whatever the personality type, every protagonist and antagonist has an **obsession**, or **MacGuffin**, that he or she wants more than anything else and is willing to do anything to get, even battle the antagonist. This passion propels each hero character along his or her journey.

Reflection and Discussion

1. It is said that everyone knows someone who would make a great film character. Who do you know? In the first "Reflection and Discussion" exercise of Chapter 1, you outlined a plot for your great story idea. Now think of interesting people you know who might integrate well with that plot. Drawing on the characteristics of those people, write a brief, one-paragraph description of who the protagonist of your story might be, along with any other principal character (e.g., love interest, buddy) and an antagonist.
2. In the previous "reflection and discussion" exercise, you identified the major plot points of the story of one of your favorite films. Now write brief character bios of the protagonist, principals, and antagonist of that movie.
3. Go to the Myers-Briggs' website, myersbriggs.org, and click around to find their typology of personality types. Which of the 16 types best describes you?

4

Theme

The third element in Aristotle's treatise is **theme**. The Greek word ***dianoia*** is also translated as "assertion," "idea," "meaning," "moral lesson," "premise," "sentiment," "thesis," and "thought." The theme is the point the dramatist wishes to convey to the audience. It is "what the play is about." It is the tenet of life that the viewers are left to ponder.

What Theme Is Not: Plot or Character

Some people, especially those just beginning to study dramatic theory, confuse theme with plot or character. When asked what the story is about (theme), they reply with what happens in the story (plot) or with a description of the protagonist and principal players (character). The theme is the moral of the story. This lesson is revealed through the characters as they progress through the plot, but the lesson is itself neither character nor plot.

Consider *La Llorona*. What is this drama really about? Some might answer: "It's about this kid who can't sleep because of the wind, and a parent tells the story of why that type of wind is called 'the weeping woman,' because a woman a long time ago had illegitimate twins and drowned them, only to feel overwhelming guilt and try to recover their bodies, but she couldn't find them so she is doomed to wander the earth, crying for her babies." That is **a plot synopsis**, not a theme. Others might answer: "It's about this woman a long time ago who drowns her illegitimate twins and pays for her act with eternal remorse and grief as she wanders the earth, crying and searching for her babies' lost bodies so she can lay them to rest." That's a brief **character description**, mixed with some plot elements, but it is not a theme.

What Theme Is: Lesson with Point of View

These brief story and character summaries do suggest the theme of *La Llorona*, however. The place to find the theme is in the protagonist's arc—the change he or she undergoes throughout the story (see Chapter 3). What is Guadalupe when we meet her? An unmarried woman who gives birth to twins. Who is she when we leave her? A lost soul wandering the earth, crying, searching for the bodies of the babies she drowned. How did she get from the beginning to the end? Guilt. Guilt for delivering bastard children into a world that condemns them and her. Guilt for trying to right the wrong of illegitimate children by murdering them. Super guilt for committing the most heinous of all crimes: infanticide. Guilt for losing the drowned bodies in the river so she can't even bury them. The broad theme of this story is guilt.

Having discovered the broad theme, let's work on the specific **lesson**—the particular treatment of that theme in this story. While every story deals with a theme that can be stated broadly in one word, such as guilt, that story also has a particular **point of view** regarding that theme. That point of view, the particular message of the drama, can be stated in a sentence rather that in just one word. Many stories are about love, for example, but the stories differ in the particular lessons they present about love: love is blind (*Shrek*, Adamson and Jenson 2001); true love conquers all (*South Pacific*, Logan 1958); love makes wise men foolish (any film with Hugh Grant), and so on.

So what is the specific theme, the full thematic statement, of *La Llorona*? Again, the answer lies in the character's progression through the story beats. What is the consequence of Guadalupe's actions? Eternal punishment. Her punishment for infanticide is the guilt, the remorse, for her action. If she were to return to the village and be forgiven and welcomed back into the fold, the theme would be about forgiveness. If she were to be tried and burned at the stake, it would be about law and justice. But her penalty is the eternal punishment of guilt. She walks the earth, neither able to live nor die, because her grief and remorse do not let her soul find rest, just as she cannot lay her babies' bodies to rest. The theme of this drama may then be stated in this way: "remorse serves as its own punishment."

Most stories explore more than one theme, too. There is always one, dominant theme, as we just discussed. However, there are other, secondary themes, as well. In the case of *La Llorona*, a secondary theme is hope. Guadalupe continues her search in the spiritual world even today, always hoping to find her murdered children. The child in the bookend story reflects this theme by choosing to be hopeful. He closes the story by saying that he believes Guadalupe "has found her babies this night." Fleshing out the one word, secondary theme of "hope" into a full thematic statement, the secondary moral of this story is: "never give up hope."

We can glean even more subthemes from this story, as well. The greatest dramatic plays, movies, and TV series can be interpreted on multiple thematic levels. Different viewers of *La Llorona* might take away different meanings, such as "society should not ruin lives by being so hypocritical and quick to condemn," or "everyone should seek forgiveness rather than live with pain," or "no matter how bad life seems, don't kill your children—it's not worth it," or "the fathers of illegitimate children should take responsibility for them," or something else. These thematic lessons might also be part of the story. Returning to the dominant theme, though, it is the protagonist's arc that suggests the primary theme: "guilt brings eternal punishment" (to state it a different way).

Another example clarifies. What is *The Wizard of Oz* (Fleming 1939) really about? Some might answer, "It's about this young girl named Dorothy and her dog Toto and this mean witch and a scarecrow and a tin man and a lion and some Munchkins and a wizard." That reply, of course, is really character, or rather a cast list. It is not theme. Others might answer, "This girl, Dorothy, and her dog run away from a mean neighbor, but Dorothy gets knocked out in a tornado and dreams about a journey to a place called Munchkinland, where she meets a scarecrow and a tin man and a lion who go with her to a place called Oz to see a wizard who can get her back home, but first she has to destroy a mean witch who wants Dorothy's slippers, and in the end she wakes up already at home." That, of course, is a plot synopsis and not a theme.

The theme, as anyone who has seen this classic film knows, is an exploration of the meaning of "home"—a theme that was especially relevant to American society in 1939, having suffered a decade of severe economic Depression that had driven many from their homes. Dorothy clearly states the full thematic lesson, or moral point, of this study of the broad theme of "home" at the end. She does not have to look any farther than her own backyard for adventure because— click your heels and say it three times out loud—"there's no place like home."

Typologies of Theme

Many of the Greek tragedies of Aristotle's time probed the theme of man's fate due to hybris, or boastful pride, and his subsequent punishment (see Chapter 3). Herman (1974) presents five universal themes in his discussion of plot patterns: love, success, vengeance, sacrifice, and family. Other typologies may include the age-old "seven deadly sins" of envy (jealousy), gluttony (excess), greed (avarice), lust (lechery), pride (hybris), sloth (laziness), and wrath (anger), or the three Biblical virtues of faith (belief), hope (trust), and love (charity) (1 Corinthians 13:13), which are sometimes combined with the classical virtues of

Seven Deadly Sins	Seven Cardinal Virtues
• Envy	• Faith
• Gluttony	• Hope
• Greed	• Love
• Lust	• Courage
• Pride	• Justice
• Sloth	• Prudence
• Wrath	• Temperance

Figure 4.1 The Seven Deadly (Cardinal) Sins versus the Seven Heavenly (Cardinal) Virtues, comprised of the four virtues of ancient Greece and the three virtues of the Holy Bible

courage (fortitude), justice (righteousness), prudence (discretion), and temperance (restraint) to create "seven cardinal virtues" that offset the "seven deadly sins" (see Figure 4.1). It may also be argued that all dramatic themes can be condensed into the general, eternal conflict between good and evil.

Treatment of Theme

What distinguishes the theme of one play from another is the specific way in which the theme is treated. In *The Wizard of Oz*, the broad theme is "home" and the specific thematic statement is that no place is better than home. In *Home Alone* (Columbus 1990), instead of the protagonist leaving for an adventure away from home only to return in the end, *à la* Dorothy, the protagonist, Kevin McCallister (Macaulay Culkin), is accidentally left at home and must defend it against two inept burglars. Again, the broad theme is "home," but here the specific treatment of that theme is that home is worth fighting for, even if your big brother beats you up and your parents accidentally forget you.

To uncover a drama's theme, ask thematic questions. Does good or evil triumph? What does the protagonist learn after undergoing the adventure? What cause and effect occurs in the story to enlighten the viewers and make them think? In answering such questions, the central idea, or point, of the play becomes clear. That is its theme. Some scholars provide additional insight on the element of theme (e.g., Armer 1989; Willis and D'Arienzo 1993).

Having already discussed *The Wizard of Oz*, another example from that same golden year of Hollywood movies, 1939, and even the same director, Victor Fleming, illustrates deeper: *Gone with the Wind*. If these two films were not adaptations of two different books, I would be tempted to argue that they could have both started out as the same pitch to two different studio executives, and then went into development and production and ended up as these two different movies. Consider this pitch in 1930s' Hollywood, which works for both films.

> A young, headstrong, country girl, disillusioned at home, sets out to satisfy her ambition in a grand, Technicolor adventure, encountering a number of interesting characters along the way, only to grow disillusioned at her adventure and return home, learning that home is the best place to be after all. The "home" theme reaches a Depression audience. At the end, the young girl drives home the theme (pun intended) by saying either "There's no place like home" or "I'll return to Tara, for tomorrow is another day."

The point is that, while these two classics share some characteristics, including theme (home), some protagonists' character traits (young girls on farms), and some elements of plot progression (leave home and return), they are obviously two very different films. One girl travels a yellow brick road with some non-human characters to a fantasy land where a good witch appears and sends her home—a fantasy film. The other girl travels the roads of America's Civil War with some all-too-human characters, including a series of husbands, to a ravished city where she loses a child to death and yet another husband to abandonment and vows to return home—a serious dramatic film. While these movies share a similar theme, their differences are in the particular ways the dramatists treat this theme in tone (fantasy v. drama) and by revealing different character dimensions and traits as their heroines move through different beats and plot points to different climaxes in their different storylines.

Experiments with Theme

As with plot and character, some dramatists explore, push, and experiment with the element of theme. Some work with themes that stretch the boundaries of what has gone before, such as new plays for the stage and screen with twists on conventional stories or relationships. Examples would be the variations on *The Wizard of Oz*, including *The Wiz* (stage musical, Smalls and Brown 1974; film, Lumet 1978) and *Wicked* (novel, Maguire 1995; stage musical, Schwarz and Holzman 2003; film, Daldry 2014). "Home is where the heart is." Another dual example is the retelling of the romantic comedy *The Taming of the Shrew* (Shakespeare 1590) in *Kiss Me Kate*, (stage musical, Porter 1948; film, Sidney 1953; various TV productions) and *10 Things I Hate about You* (film, Junger 1999; TV series 2009–2010) (see Chapter 8, Figure 8.1). "Love conquers all." Even when adapting, altering, experimenting, and pushing boundaries, dramatists still make statements about life with their stories, no matter how new or unusual those stories might be. These life statements are their themes.

Some might try to write stories without themes. This text posits that this is impossible, both in theory and in practice. Attempting to write drama with no theme by definition addresses the theme of there being no theme, or perhaps the theme of rebellion against the dramatic norm of theme. The popular situation comedy *Seinfeld* (1990–1998) was heralded for being "a show about nothing." Of course, that "nothingness" itself was the theme. In particular, the program poked fun at the banality of the characters' mundane pastimes and narcissistic attempts at immediate gratification that prevented them from having any serious relationships or employment. By extension, the writers poked fun at us and our collective conscious in the 1990s. So this famous television comedy about nothing was really a comedy about something: the mundane banality—the nothingness—of everyday life, which in this case led to wondrous laughter.

Sometimes a dramatist is so drawn to a theme that he or she creates a number of works that explore that theme from different perspectives. Peter Shaffer is an example. He wrote, among other things, the stage plays and then screenplays for *Equus* (stage play, 1973; film, Lumet 1977) and *Amadeus* (stage play, 1979; film, Forman 1984). Both explore the themes of passion colliding with mediocrity and society's expectations of normality. In *Equus*, a psychiatrist, Martin Dysart—the normal one who follows society's rules—confronts a young man, Alan Strang—the passionate one beyond society's rules—who had sex in a horse stall and, overcome by guilt, blinded the horses in a fit of rage. In *Amadeus*, a court composer, Salieri—the normal one—confronts a young man, Mozart—the passionate one—who is vulgar and crass and yet has been gifted by God as the superior composer. In both plays and movies, the normal one (psychiatrist, court composer) reveals his jealousy for the passionate one (horse-blinder, vulgar musician). Both normal ones long to experience life with the passion of the other ones, but they have chosen to conform to society's rules and, therefore, have become merely mediocre.

Though these two stories and their characters are different, occurring in different countries and centuries, both question social norms and the quality of life with and without passion. In the clash of society's restraint of passion—which can harm—against an individual's unbridled passion—which can also harm, the theme of the dramas is revealed. They are about passion, specifically the need to sacrifice a lust for life to harness passion and bring it within accepted social boundaries. This theme can be stated as a paradox: "Restrained passion leads to mediocrity, while unbridled passion leads to ruin." The viewer is left to ponder, "Which do I choose?" Hopefully, we can all find a happy middle ground, living passionately without destroying ourselves or others.

Summary

Every story has a theme: a point of view or moral lesson it illustrates. Themes are not plot summaries or character descriptions. Rather, themes are discovered in the relationship and progression, or arc, of the protagonist and antagonist throughout the story, culminating in a climax that reveals the point. Different typologies of theme are useful in identifying the broad, brushstroke themes of stories, which can be stated with single words, such as love, hate, jealousy, revenge, greed, and so on. Each story also treats its broad theme in a specific way, providing a particular lesson, or thematic statement, within that broader thematic context. Even stories that push the boundaries of theme have a point of view or moral lesson for the viewers to consider. One final and well-known example illustrates theme. Aesop's fable *The Tortoise and the Hare* (*c.* 500 BCE) is about competition: a race between a turtle and a rabbit that represents the broader competitions we all face in life. Because the methodical but slower tortoise beats the stop-and-start but faster hare, the specific thematic statement regarding competition is (you know this one): "slow and steady wins the race" (see Figure 4.2).

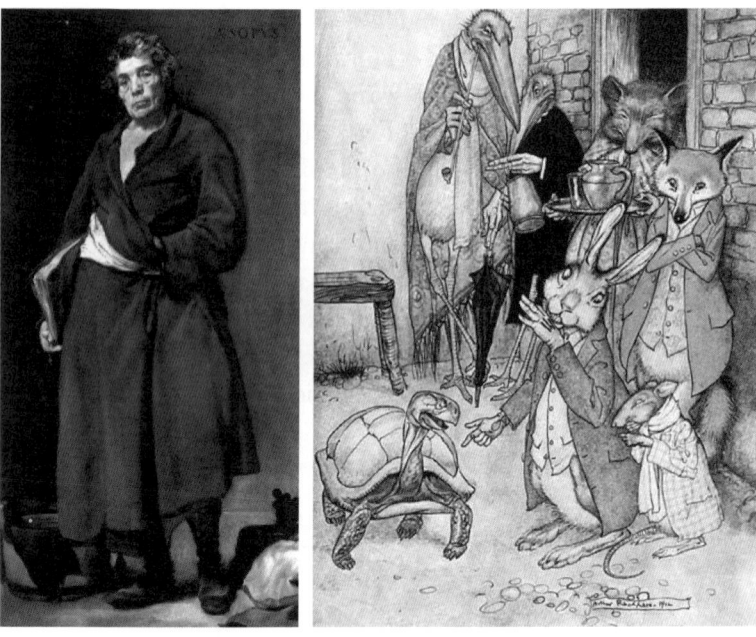

Figure 4.2 Aesop (c. 620–564 BCE) and an illustration of his famous fable, *The Tortoise and the Hare*

Reflection and Discussion

1. In the "Reflection and Discussion" sections of the previous chapters, you began to outline a story and characters. Now suppose you are told that you have five minutes to live. In those remaining minutes, you are taken to a mountaintop with a loudspeaker that reaches to the ends of the earth. You have this one opportunity to tell the world the most important lesson you have learned in your life so far. What is it? What would you yell from that mountaintop for the whole world to hear? This is a major theme in your life. Now, adjust and revise your great story idea and characters to envelop that life lesson.
2. Think again of your favorite film from the previous "reflection and discussion" sections. Can you state that film's major thematic

lesson in one sentence? What secondary themes does the film explore?
3. Suppose the hare had won the race in Aesop's fable. What do you think the theme would be then? Make up different versions of the story, using different plot points along different race courses, with different supporting characters, different dialogue, and so on. How do these different elements inform different themes?

5

Dialogue

The fourth of Aristotle's dramatic elements is **dialogue**. Other translations from the Greek *lexis* include "diction," "language," "lexicon," "speech," and "words." Dialogue is the word choice and speech construction dramatists create for their characters. It is "what the characters say." Without dialogue, the dramatist creates mime—a different form of expression in which the story and characters are advanced through visual performance only.

Show, Don't Tell

Before talkies, there were silent films, which were never really silent because they were accompanied by live music in the Nickelodeons and theaters that were large enough to hire at least a pianist or organist, or maybe even a trio or quartet or an orchestra. Filmmakers in this "silent" era perfected a visual language of film, including the use of wide shots to establish location, followed by medium shots to reveal action and close-up shots to show emotion, along with juxtaposing shots to change the viewers' perspective and create associations between characters and action, and editing different scenes into a complete story that crosses time and place. Obviously, these "silent" stories were told with far less "talk" than today. Brief dialogue was displayed on title cards intercut with the visual action, but the bulk of a story's progression was told in its action (Bordwell and Thompson 2010; Cook 2008; Phillips 2009; Wexman 2009).

Today, screenplays, whether for the jumbo, large, medium, small, or micro screen, contain much more dialogue. The characters' words, in addition to action, move the story, reveal back story, and enlighten characters. Still, because film is a visual medium, the old adage applies to writing: "Show, don't tell"; or "Don't tell us if you can show us." At its best, dialogue in drama (serious or comic) benefits from **economy of writing**, not **overwriting**. It is efficient, accomplishing its purpose with few words. Actions and behaviors do the rest. Drama, whether on stage or screen, is a visual medium of expressing emotions and ideas, so the audience deserves and expects to *see* the story unfold, not just *hear* it.

Consider the "life montage" in Act 1 of *Up* (Docter and Peterson 2009). Without dialogue, we watch the progression of Carl Fredrickson's (Ed Asner) life with his wife, from marriage through the loss of a child to her death. To be sure, we could hear Carl narrate this story, revealing how happy he was with Elle until the child died, leaving a hole in his heart that will soon be filled by the unlikely Russell, and how he never got to take his wife to Paradise Falls, and that he misses her so much he cannot let the house go with all its memories of her. While that would work, the silent montage manages to tell all this in motion image only, setting up the rest of the story with its action rather than words. The montage shows us Carl's life leading up to the present, rather than telling us. It must be noted that, like in the silent movies before it, this scene is accompanied by music, as is the case with nearly every movie montage. In this example, the nostalgic melody heightens the nostalgia of the life Carl once had, enhancing the silent visual imagery of the montage.

Creating Dialogue

While it is important for screenwriters to show action that reveals character and progresses story, it is equally important for today's screenwriters to write dialogue. The definition of dialogue given previously is simple; however, the creation of dialogue is not always so. It can be a complex and creative process, involving many considerations. It can also be great fun! Some writers enjoy writing alone; others find it valuable to write with a partner. Television series employ **staff writers**, from 2 to 12 scribes (more or less, depending on the scope of the show). Using writing partners, however many, allows the authors to become the voices of different characters in the story. The writing team can banter back and forth, giving words to the characters, generating dialogue naturally among each other, rather than in isolation.

Whether alone or with others, writers enjoy climbing into their characters' heads—if they have created interesting and engaging characters. As they inhabit those characters, they begin to speak in those characters' voices, producing those characters' dialogue. Often, the first pass of brainstorming dialogue in the persons of the story's characters does not result in the final, polished words, but that creative process does get words on the page. Then in the **rewriting** phase of the screenplay (e.g., Selbo 2008), the author can polish the dialogue, cutting parts that do not work to move the story or reveal character in the end, and enhancing and fine-tuning just those parts that are necessary for the story.

Poeticism

The resulting dialogue may be heightened: more poetic than realistic to fit dramatic styles that call for speech that is not everyday. This **poeticism** can be found, for example, in the plays of the ancient Greek dramatists (see Figure 5.1). In Sophocles' *Oedipus Rex* (*c.* 429 BCE), for instance, Oedipus blinds himself and banishes himself from the Kingdom of Thebes to end the curse that he himself has brought on the land. The chorus—a device used in ancient Greek plays—closes the drama with these poetic words:

> You residents of Thebes, our native land,
> look on this man, this Oedipus, the one
> who understood that celebrated riddle.
> He was the most powerful of men.
> All citizens who witnessed this man's wealth
> were envious. Now what a surging tide

Figure 5.1 The "big three" ancient Greek tragedians, Aeschylus (c. 525–455 BCE), Sophocles (496–406 BCE), and Euripides (c. 480–406 BCE), with Sophocles' most famous creation, *Oedipus the King* (c. 429 BCE).

of terrible disaster sweeps around him.
So while we wait to see that final day, we cannot call a mortal being
happy before he's passed beyond life free from pain.
(From classic-enotes.com=http://www.classic-enotes.com/drama/sophocles/oedipus-rex/full-text-of-oedipus-rex/)

Naturalism

Dialogue may also be more realistic than poetic, which is generally more appropriate for dramatic styles that represent slices of life. Extreme realism is called **naturalism**. The films of Quentin Tarantino are known for their naturalistic dialogue, with characters sometimes rambling on about the simplest things, just like in real life. In *Pulp Fiction* (1994), for example, two hired assassins, Vincent Vega (John Travolta) and Jules Winnfield (Samuel Jackson) pass the time in the car by talking about hamburgers in Europe:

VINCENT: . . . In Paris, you can buy a beer in McDonald's. And you know what they call a Quarter Pounder with Cheese in Paris?
JULES: They don't call it a Quarter Pounder with Cheese?
VINCENT: No man, they got the metric system. They wouldn't know what the f— a quarter pounder is.
JULES: Then what do they call it?
VINCENT: They call it a Royale with Cheese.
JULES: Royale with Cheese.
VINCENT: That's right.
JULES: What do they call a Big Mac?
VINCENT: Big Mac's a Big Mac, but they call it Le Big Mac.
JULES: Le Big Mac. [laughs] What do they call a Whopper?
VINCENT: I don't' know. I didn't go into Burger King.

Even naturalistic dialogue like this should serve a purpose, of course. In this case, it sets up the scene in which the two shake down and kill their target, but not before Jules eats the young man's cheeseburger.

Realism

Some dramatic scripts may call for a style of realism that is not completely naturalistic, but more tightly written—more efficient in its word use. This middle ground of **realism** is appropriate to much film and television content. Characters speak fairly realistic dialogue, but it is edited to just those words necessary for the characters to move the story forward. For example, David Mamet is known for dialogue that is both realistic and efficient in his plays and films. Conversation is true-to-life, but words are not wasted. In one example from *The Untouchables* (De Palma 1987), federal agent Eliot Ness (Kevin Costner) speaks with veteran Chicago cop Jim Malone (Sean Connery) about Ness' mission to get Al Capone (Robert De Niro).

MALONE: You said you wanted to get Capone. Do you really wanna get him? You see what I'm saying is, what are you prepared to do?
NESS: Anything within the law.
MALONE: And then what are you prepared to do? If you open the can on these worms, you must be prepared to go all the way. Because they're not gonna give up the fight until one of you is dead.
NESS: I want to get Capone! I don't know how to do it.
MALONE: You wanna know how to get Capone? They pull a knife, you pull a gun. He sends one of yours to the hospital, you send one of his to the morgue. That's the Chicago way! And that's how you get Capone. Now do you want to do that? Are you ready to do that? I'm offering you a deal. Do you want this deal?
NESS: I have sworn to capture this man with all legal powers at my disposal and I will do so.

MALONE: Well, the Lord hates a coward. [They shake.] Do you know what a blood oath is, Mr. Ness?
NESS: Yes.
MALONE: Good, 'cause you just took one.

While this dialogue is realistic, it is tightly written, with no rambling discourse (as in the more naturalistic *Pulp Fiction*). It is rather efficient and to the point, revealing only what we need to know at this point in the story.

Another example illustrates the point of tight but realistic dialogue. *Chinatown* (Polanski 1974) is considered a must-see film for film buffs. Detective Jake Gittes (Jack Nicholson) unravels a murder mystery involving Los Angeles water rights. Near the end, he confronts the perpetrator, Noah Cross (John Huston), who had an incestuous relationship with his daughter Evelyn (Faye Dunaway), producing a girl who is both Cross' daughter and granddaughter. Writer Robert Towne pens this exchange:

GITTES: How much are you worth?
CROSS: I have no idea. How much do you want?
GITTES: I want to know what you're worth. Over ten million?
CROSS: Oh, my, yes.
GITTES: Then why are you doing it? How much better can you eat? What can you buy that you can't already afford?
CROSS: The future, Mr Gittes. The future. Now where's the girl? I want the only daughter I have left. As you found out, Evelyn was lost to me a long time ago.
GITTES: (with sarcasm) Who do you blame for that? Her?
CROSS: I don't blame myself. You see, Mr Gittes, most people never have to face the fact that at the right time and right place, they're capable of anything.

Here a few lines of dialogue reveal much about the characters and what has happened in the story. Gittes is a man both curious about and sickened by Cross. Cross is filled with greed and can even justify incest to himself. These lines come near the end of the story at the moment the audience, along with detective Gittes, needs to know Cross' motivation. Along with his motivation, we learn Cross' callous perspective of the lives he has ruined with his greed, and we see Gittes' strength in confronting this tyrant.

Heightened Realism

Some stories might benefit from dialogue that, while still realistic, is closer to "poetic" than to "naturalistic." That is, the dialogue, while representing the way humans speak, is not wholly true-to-life conversation, but a more stylized version of speech. Consider the scripts of brothers Joel and Ethan Coen. The Coen brothers' films are renowned for characters with wonderful quirks and inner contradictions. Their idiosyncrasies are often revealed in dialogue that, while usually realistic and not poetic (at least not always formally poetic in rhyme and meter), is rather heightened in its style. In *Raising Arizona* (1987), H.I. McDunnough (Nicolas Cage) and his wife Edwina (Holly Hunter) steal a baby because they cannot have one of their own, but in the end, they return the baby to its family. "H.I.," who is a common convenience store robber, reflects on what has happened with this closing voice-over that is realistic but close to poetic—a heightened realism that contradicts the simple character:

> That night I had a dream. I dreamt I was as light as the ether, a floatin' spirit, visitin' things to come. The shades and shadows of the people in my life wrestled their way into my slumber. I dreamt that Gale and Evelle had decided to return to prison. Probably that's just as well. I don't mean to sound superior, and they're a swell coupla guys, but maybe they weren't ready yet to come out into the world [visually at this point the two jailbreaker characters literally climb back into the muddy tunnel

from which they escaped prison—returning to the womb of incarceration because they can't deal with the outside world].

And then I dreamed on, into the future, to a Christmas morning in the Arizona home, where Nathan Junior [the baby] was openin' a present from a kindly couple who preferred to remain unknown [H.I. and Edwina]. I saw Glen a few years later, still havin' no luck gettin' the cops to listen to his wild tales about me and Ed. Maybe he threw in one Polack joke too many. I don't know.

But still I dreamed on, further into the future than I'd ever dreamed before, watchin' Nathan Junior's progress from afar, takin' pride in his accomplishments, as if he were our own, wonderin' if he ever thought of us, and hopin' that maybe we'd broadened his horizons a little, even if he couldn't remember just how they got broadened.

But still I hadn't dreamt nothin' about me and Ed, until the end. And this was cloudier, because it was years, years away. But I saw an old couple bein' visited by their children and all their grandchildren, too. The old couple weren't screwed up, and neither were their kids or their grandkids. And I don't know, you tell me, this whole dream, was it wishful thinkin'? Was I just fleein' reality, like I know I'm liable to do? But me and Ed, we can be good, too. And it seemed real. It seemed like us. And it seemed like, well . . . our home. If not Arizona, then a land not too far away, where all parents are strong and wise and capable, and all the children are happy and beloved. I don't know. Maybe it was Utah.

Here, it seems unlikely that a common petty thief would have the education, or vocabulary, to wax so eloquently about his dream of a future life. This heightened monologue adds to the engaging contradictions of this character.

Functions of Dialogue

Whatever style the dialogue is, from poetic to heightened realistic to realistic to naturalistic, it has three functions in drama: *advance the plot, reveal character traits*, and *point to the theme*.

Advance Plot

Screenwriters move their stories along with both dialogue and action. The previous example of Carl's nostalgic life montage in *Up* is an example of the visual action advancing a story. Dialogue, too, is often used to progress through one scene to the next. For example, in the television series *Mission Impossible* (1966–1973), as well as in the film franchise (Paramount), the protagonist receives his mission in the form of dialogue, specifically an audio recording, that self-destructs after explaining this mission. This dialogue recording sets the new mission in motion.

Reveal Character

Dialogue and action also reveal character traits. Again, the montage in *Up* illustrates how action—in this case a visual montage—can show much about character. Regarding dialogue that reveals character, a personal favorite, *Being John Malkovich* (Jonze 1999), offers an example. A puppeteer, Craig Schwartz (John Cusack), discovers a portal into the mind of actor John Malkovich (himself) and sets up shop with associate Maxine Lund (Catherine Keener), charging a fee to customers to be inside John Malkovich. A sad and fat man arrives, Erroll (W. Earl Brown).

ERROLL: Hello, I'm here about the ad.
CRAIG: Please, have a seat.
ERROLL: When you say I can be somebody else, what do you mean exactly?

CRAIG: Exactly that. We can put you inside someone else's body for 15 minutes.

ERROLL: Oh, this is just the medical breakthrough I've been waiting for. Are there any side effects? Please say no! Please say no!

MAXINE: No.

ERROLL: Long-term psychic or physiological repercussions?

MAXINE: No. Don't be an ass.

ERROLL: Can I be anyone I want?

MAXINE: You can be John Malkovich.

ERROLL: Well that's perfect. My second choice. Ah, this is wonderful. Too good to be true! You see, I'm a sad man. Sad and fat and alone. Oh, I've tried all the diets, my friends. Lived for a year on nothing but imitation mayonnaise. Did it work? You be the judge. But Malkovich! King of New York! Man about town! Most eligible bachelor! Bon Vivant! The Schopenhauer of the twentieth century! Thin man extraordinaire!

MAXINE: Two hundred dollars, please.

ERROLL: Yes. Yes. A thousand times, yes!

Although the character of Erroll is only in this scene and a brief scene that follows when he exits the portal alongside a freeway, this dialogue reveals the person he is.

Point to Theme

A third function of both action and dialogue is to point to the theme. Again using *Up* as an example, the visual montage reveals Carl's happy life with Elle and his resulting sorrow at her loss, so much so that the house is all he has left of her, setting up his inability to let the house (the past) go and embrace today. The previous example of *The Wizard of Oz* serves to illustrate how dialogue also points to theme. Glinda the Good Witch tells Dorothy that she "always had the power to go back to Kansas," but that she wouldn't have believed her earlier. "She had to learn it for herself." Dorothy then states what she has learned: "Well, I—I think that it—that it wasn't enough just to want to see Uncle Henry and Auntie Em—and it's that—if I ever go looking for my heart's desire again, I won't look any further than my own backyard. Because if it isn't there, I never really lost it to begin with! Is that right?" To which Glinda replies, "That's all it is." Moments later, Dorothy utters her famous thematic line, "There's no place like home."

Dialogue does not have to perform just one function at a time; to the contrary, efficient dialogue often performs two or all three of these functions simultaneously. In *Finding Nemo* (Stanton and Unkrich 2003), Marlin (Albert Brooks) finds himself inside a whale's mouth with his ally Dory (Ellen DeGeneres), clinging to the whale's tongue to keep from being swallowed. Dory speaks "whale" to the big mammal, but Marlin chastises her.

MARLIN: You can't speak whale!
DORY: Yes I can!
MARLIN: No you can't. You think you can do these things, but you can't, Nemo. [He realizes he said "Nemo" instead of "Dory"; the whale bellows.]
DORY: All right. [She lets go and falls; Marlin grabs her.]
MARLIN: Dory!
DORY: He said it's time to let go. Everything's gonna be all right.
MARLIN: How do you know? How do you know something bad isn't gonna happen?
DORY: I don't!
[Marlin lets go. They plunge downward together toward the belly of the beast. Suddenly the whale spouts them from its blow hole into the harbor.]

Here, the dialogue *moves the plot* by getting Marlin to follow Dory's lead and let go so they can be spewed into Sydney Harbor, moving closer to their goal of finding Nemo. The dialogue also *reveals character*: optimistic Dory, thinking she can speak whale, is fearlessly ready to follow what she thinks the whale is saying—to let go; however, pessimistic Marlin resists, fearing they will be swallowed by the great beast. In the end, he decides to let go, too, showing that he is moving along his arc—ultimately, he must let go of his son. The dialogue *points to the film's theme*, as well. Marlin learns the moral lesson to show his love for his son by no longer being overprotective but letting him go live his own life. At the film's end, back on the coral reef, Nemo heads off for school, but comes back to give Marlin a hug and say, "Love you, Dad." Marlin hugs Nemo back, saying, "I love you too, son." He holds on a bit long, though, prompting Nemo to say, "Uh, Dad, you can let go now." Marlin lets go and says, "Sorry. Now go have an adventure!"

Comprehensibility

Whatever the style and function of dialogue, it must be comprehensible above all else. **Comprehensibility** is key because if the viewers are unable to follow what is spoken, they leave saying, "I couldn't understand anything," rather than reveling in the catharsis of the moment. To be sure, a writer might create a bit of incomprehensible dialogue to make a point about a character who cannot speak clearly, either dramatically in the case of, say, a stroke victim, or comically in the case of, say, a western hayseed who speaks "authentic frontier gibberish" for laughs (*Blazing Saddles*, Brooks 1974). These story exceptions noted, the audience must be able to comprehend the words that the characters speak. Smiley (2006) cites six additional characteristics of good dramatic dialogue: clarity, interest, appropriateness, economy, liveliness, and rhythm. Each of these is important in attracting and holding an audience. Other scholars offer additional perspective on dialogue (e.g., Hunter 2004; Morley 2008; Rilla 1973; Stempel 1982).

Let's consider the dialogue in *La Llorona*. There isn't much. Because video is a visual medium, a good deal of the story and character revelation is described in action lines, not dialogue lines. Still, there is some dialogue. It is deliberately simple: everyday words and sentence structure make it comprehensible. It advances the plot: the "bookend" story is set up with a child's cries for a parent, who then enters the child's room and tells the story within this story. That story-within-a-story is set up with the old hag's dialogue, announcing the birth of twins to Guadalupe and their curse of illegitimacy. The dialogue also reveals character: the child at the open is frightened by the wind, and in the end is hopeful that Guadalupe has finally found her babies. The parent's words reveal a loving, compassionate nature, reinforcing Guadalupe's compassion for her children while also contrasting with her murderous deed. The dialogue also points to theme. The parent's explanation for the sound of a sorrowful wind is Guadalupe's eternal punishment: that wind is Guadalupe crying as her remorseful soul wanders the earth in search of her lost babies.

Shakespeare (1564–1616) serves as another example (see Figure 5.2). Many first-time readers of his plays complain that they cannot understand the dialogue. This lack of comprehension turns many people away. However, as readers become familiar with Shakespeare and are able to understand his words, they often marvel at the mastery

Figure 5.2 William Shakespeare (1564–1616) and his most famous creation, *Hamlet* (1603)

of his dialogue. In time, Shakespeare's writing becomes clear. It is interesting, appropriate, lively, rhythmic, and at times even economical. In his expert passages, readers discover just how contemporary Shakespeare's stories, characters, and themes are—revealed in his dialogue as well as his action.

Consider that most famous soliloquy from that most famous tragedy, *Hamlet* (1603) (see Figure 5.2). Hamlet must avenge his father's death by killing the murderer, his uncle, the king, but how? Pondering suicide as a way out of his misery in Act III scene 1, the Prince of Denmark reflects in poetic iambic pentameter:

> To be, or not to be: that is the question:
> Whether 'tis nobler in the mind to suffer
> The slings and arrows of outrageous fortune,
> Or to take arms against a sea of troubles,
> And by opposing end them? To die: to sleep;
> No more; and by a sleep to say we end
> The heart-ache and the thousand natural shocks
> That flesh is heir to, 'tis a consummation
> Devoutly to be wish'd. To die, to sleep; To sleep:
> perchance to dream: ay, there's the rub;
> For in that sleep of death what dreams may come
> When we have shuffled off this mortal coil,
> Must give us pause: there's the respect
> That makes calamity of so long life.

Here, Shakespeare pens some mighty poetry to give his audience a feast for the ears while revealing the inner conflict and suicidal thoughts of his protagonist.

Now consider the animated film, *The Lion King* (Allers and Minkoff 1994), which has many of the same story, character, and thematic elements as *Hamlet*. Realizing that some readers might take umbrage at my comparing *Hamlet* with a Disney movie, I can only ask your indulgence. Like Hamlet, Simba (Matthew Broderick) runs from his past. Like Hamlet, his uncle has killed his father, the king, thereby usurping the throne. Simba's childhood friend finds him and attempts to persuade him to return home to avenge his father's murder by taking his rightful throne back, but Simba leaves her, expressing his inner conflict with straightforward prose rather than iambic pentameter:

> She's wrong. I can't go back. What would it prove, anyway? It won't change anything. You can't change the past. [Looks up at the stars to his father.] You said you'd always be there for me! But you're not. And it's because of me. It's my fault. It's my fault.

Here, we see how dialogue can be very different in style and content while serving essentially the same function. In these two examples, the different historical eras and target audiences require different writing to be comprehensible. Shakespeare was writing for seventeenth-century, adult theater goers, so flowery poetry that heightens the dialogue (a monologue in this example) is appropriate for Hamlet when he contemplates whether or not to go on. Likewise, Disney targets children with its contemporary animated films, so it is appropriate to have a talking lion speak in simple prose when he struggles with his decision whether or not to face his destiny or continue to hide from it.

Memorable Lines

What dialogue in what films or television shows do you remember best? What is the first line that pops into your head? Now consider why you remember that line of dialogue. Perhaps it made you laugh, such as, "When I'm good, I'm very good, but when I'm bad, I'm better" (Mae West in *I'm No Angel* 1933). Perhaps it made you cry, such as, "E.T., phone home" (E.T. in *E.T. the Extra-Terrestrial* 1982). Perhaps it built tension, such as, "Go ahead, make my day" (Clint Eastwood in *Dirty Harry* 1971). Perhaps it was a simple understatement, such as, "You're gonna need a bigger boat" (Roy Scheider in *Jaws* 1975). Perhaps it spoke a truth, such as, "The list is life" (Ben Kingsley in *Schindler's List* 1993). Perhaps it was a long time in coming, such as, "Frankly, my dear, I don't give a damn" (Clark Gable in *Gone with the Wind* 1939). Perhaps it expressed something you've always wanted to say, such as, "I'm as mad as hell, and I'm not going to take this anymore!" (Peter Finch in *Network* 1976). Perhaps it was the perfect catchphrase, such as, "Show me the money!" (Cuba Gooding Jr.), or the perfect romantic statement, such as, "You complete me" (Tom Cruise) or "You had me at hello" (Renée Zellweger, all three in *Jerry Maguire* 1996).

Even more than *Jerry Maguire*, there's *Casablanca* (Curtiz, 1942) (see Figure 5.3). This film is considered to have the most quotable lines of dialogue from any film. Humphrey Bogart gets most of them: "Of all the gin joints in all the towns in all the world, she walks into mine"; "If that plane leaves the ground and you're not with him, you'll regret it; maybe not today; maybe not tomorrow; but soon and for the rest of your life"; "We'll always have Paris"; "I'm no good at

Figure 5.3 Rick Blaine (Humphrey Bogart) and Ilsa Lund (Ingrid Bergman) in *Casablanca* (Curtiz 1942)

being noble, but it doesn't take much to see that the problems of three little people don't amount to a hill of beans in this crazy world"; "Here's looking at you, kid"; "Louis, I think this is the beginning of a beautiful friendship." Others get some memorable lines, too: Ingrid Bergman, "Play it once, Sam, for old time's sake" (also "Play it, Sam" and "Play it again," which are often combined into "Play it again, Sam," though that exact line is not spoken); and Claude Raines, "I'm shocked, shocked to find that gambling is going on in here," and "Round up the usual suspects."

Many writers are happy just to finish a screenplay, thrilled if it sells, ecstatic if it gets made, and beyond words if people remember any of it. The screenwriters of *Casablanca*—Julius Epstein, Philip Epstein, and Howard Koch—must be over the stars in the next life having penned all these quotations that entered the common vocabulary. A rhetorical question to ponder is why are all these lines from this one film so memorable? I would suggest that their brevity carries deeper meaning and emotion at just the right moments, those moments being set up with great storytelling craft so that only a few words are needed. Of course, having Humphrey Bogart, Ingrid Bergman, and Claude Raines deliver those lines also helps.

The lines we remember are usually short, to the point, fit the situation and character perfectly, and have deeper meaning. Stating the meaning literally would require more words. Memorable dialogue uses words sparsely. If the moment in the story is set up well, those few words carry a larger meaning. For example, consider this famous line: "Make him an offer he can't refuse" (Marlon Brando in *The Godfather* 1972). What Brando's mafia character is really saying is, "Tell him if he does not accept our terms, we will hurt or kill him in some gruesome, painful, bloody way." Too many words, but all of them are implied in the much shorter and sweeter, "Make him an offer he can't refuse." We know what those words mean because they have been set up. We know the character who speaks them is a mob boss and his son, earlier in the film, tells his girlfriend that his father can be very persuasive by making people offers they can't refuse, explaining that this means he kills them.

Dual Meaning

The words people speak often have two levels of meaning: the **literal meaning** of the words and the **intended meaning** they imply. Have you ever been on a date and been offered dessert, which you really wanted, but said "no," hoping your date would coax you into ordering some, anyway? Literally, "no" means, "No, I do not want dessert." But in this case, "no" means, "Yes, I would love some dessert, but I don't want to seem like a pig, so I'll say the opposite of what I mean, hoping you'll pick up on that and continue to entice me so I can demure a few more times to appear polite and eventually give in, blaming you for my sweet tooth." Too many words. A simple "no" can mean all that, if this restaurant scene in your life is set up properly with some back story (exposition, flashback, etc.) about your weakness for sweets, coupled with your desire to do what is socially acceptable on a date.

So it is with the best dialogue in comedy and drama on the stage and screen. The intended meaning, or **subtext**, is often hidden beneath the literal words. "If you build it, he will come" (*Field of Dreams* 1989). What is "it" and who is "he"? Literally, this is a riddle—a great way to set up a story by planting something (pun intended—Iowa corn field) that the viewers want to see solved, so they stick around for the payoff. Getting beneath the riddle, Ray Kinsella (Kevin Costner) becomes inspired to build a baseball diamond in a corn field (the "it") so ball players from the past can reunite and play, eventually joined by Ray's late father (the "he"). On yet a deeper level of meaning, "it" is Ray's dream, symbolized by the ball diamond, and "he" is the hero Ray never got to know, represented generally by the ball players, then personified in his deceased father. All that in seven words! How awful and unmemorable the film would be if the whispering voice said, "Construct a baseball diamond in a corn field so that the Chicago

White Sox players who threw the 1919 World Series can come and play, and in so doing you will realize your dream to know your father."

Summary

When possible, screenwriters should create scenes with **action** that shows the story instead of **dialogue** that tells the story. However, when used appropriately, dialogue can be as effective as action in storytelling. When dialogue is the best choice, whether *serious* or *comic*, it should be *economical* and *sparse*—not *overwritten* but used only when necessary, motivated by and appropriate to **character** and action. Writers may work alone or with a partner or team of **staff writers**, allowing different writers to become the **voices** of different characters. Whether alone or with someone else, writers create dialogue that may fall anywhere on the continuum from **poetic** to **heightened realism** to **realism** to **naturalism**.

Dialogue should accomplish one or more of three functions: *advance the plot, reveal characters*, and *point to the theme*. To accomplish these functions, spoken words must be **comprehensible** to their audience; otherwise, the viewers are lost and confused. The most memorable lines of dialogue are *brief*, to the point, fit the character and action perfectly, and carry *deeper meaning* and *emotion* at just the right time. Much effective dialogue has **dual meanings**: the **literal** words and the **subtext** they imply.

Reflection and Discussion

1. In the previous "Reflection and Discussion" exercises, you considered a major theme that you have learned in your life and created a plot and characters to demonstrate it. Now, write lines of dialogue for the principal characters whose words illustrate that moral point. Then combine the words, characters, and plot to create a scene with both action and dialogue that makes your thematic point of view clear.

2. Team up with a writing partner who shares your favorite television or web series. You both need to know the characters. Divide the principals between you, each taking one or more of the main characters. Now banter back and forth as those characters, writing a few pages of a **spec script** for that show—a script written on "speculation" rather than a commissioned script written on "assignment." Do you enjoy brainstorming dialogue with a writing partner? Did the exercise help you write faster and better, or did it hinder you?
3. Here are a few lines of dialogue from Samuel Beckett's best-known, minimalist, absurdist, tragicomedy *Waiting for Godot* (1953). Consider different meanings these lines could have. Add some description and back story to create scenes in which this dialogue means those different things. Allow the characters to be either male or female or one each. Could they be two simpletons standing on the side of a road waiting for someone or something who will never come (the literal setting and meaning in the play)? Could they be spies talking in code? Could they be lovers coming on to each other with these words as foreplay? Could the opposite be the case—two lovers breaking up? What other subtexts can you create for these words?

ESTRAGON: I'm asking you if we're tied.
VLADIMIR: Tied?
ESTRAGON: Ti-ed.
VLADIMIR: How do you mean tied?
ESTRAGON: Down.
VLADIMIR: But to whom? By whom?
ESTRAGON: To your man.
VLADIMIR: To Godot? Tied to Godot! What an idea! No question of it. For the moment.

ESTRAGON: His name is Godot?
VLADIMIR: I think so.
ESTRAGON: Fancy that. Funny, the more you eat the worse it gets.
VLADIMIR: With me it's just the opposite.
ESTRAGON: In other words?
VLADIMIR: I get used to the muck as I go along.
ESTRAGON: Is that the opposite?
VLADIMIR: Question of temperament.
ESTRAGON: Of character.
VLADIMIR: Nothing you can do about it.
ESTRAGON: No use struggling.
VLADIMIR: One is what one is.
ESTRAGON: No use wriggling.
VLADIMIR: The essential doesn't change.
ESTRAGON: Nothing to be done.

6

Sound

Aristotle discusses **music** as the fifth element in the *Poetics*. The Greek ***melos*** is also translated as "melody" and "song." In the context of today's film, television, and theater, **sound** is a more relevant term than music because it is broader. It encompasses music as well as sound effects and voice—all the aural elements of drama. For this reason, I expand Aristotle's discussion to include not only music but the other sound elements in dramatic productions: sound effects and voice. The total audio package is "what the play sounds like."

Sound for Screenwriters

Why include a chapter on sound in this primer about story structure? Screenwriters must know all the elements that comprise the art form for which they are writing: motion image with sound. Sound is divided into three categories: **voice**, **sound effects**, and **music**. In fact, those working in the motion picture sound crafts tend to specialize as recordists, editors, and/or mixers in one of these three categories. From the writing perspective, voice, sound effects, and music can reveal character, advance the plot, and point to theme. For this reason, writers must know the basics of these three elements to incorporate them effectively in their stories.

That noted, screen authors should *not overwrite* music, sound, and vocal cues. The director has the final say regarding a film's soundtrack. The composer ultimately scores and records the music. The sound effects' team ultimately generates and mixes all the necessary sounds. The casting director ultimately selects actors with appropriate vocal characteristics. For this reason, a screenwriter should *not* describe every time background music fades in and out, or every time footsteps are needed for a walking-talking scene, sometimes called a **walkie-talkie**, or every time an actor should raise or lower his or her voice. These details are determined by others.

However, when a particular piece of music or a particular sound or a particular vocal characteristic is necessary to the story or to a character, then and only then should the writer include that in the screenplay. For example, in *La Llorona*, the sound effect of a mournful wind is necessary in the script because that is the sound of the weeping woman that sets the story in motion and serves as the play's title. Regarding voice, in any **biopic**—a "biographical picture" that is **narrative** rather than **documentary**, based on incidents in the life of an actual person (e.g., *Ray* [Charles], Hackford 2004; [Truman] *Capote*, Miller 2005; [Cesar] *Chavez*, Luna 2013)—the vocal characteristics of the actor should be described in a way that at least resembles the speech of the actual person for authenticity. In the sound category of music, the choice of Mozart's opera *Don Giovanni* in *Amadeus* (Forman 1984) is necessary to the script because it is in that opera that Salieri (F. Murray Abraham) realizes Mozart (Tom Hulce) has conjured up his dead father, giving Salieri the idea of how to ruin Mozart.

Music

Beginning with Aristotle's notion of music, this element of a production's soundtrack can greatly heighten emotion, drawing the viewers into the story, and leading them to that final feeling of satisfaction, or catharsis (see Chapter 8). Music can also be part of the story: a device to reveal character and advance plot. Because music can give life to a production, some scholars (e.g., Timm 2003) assert that music is the "soul" of cinema. This was as true during the so-called silent era of film as it is today (see Chapter 5). Silent films (see Figure 6.1) were often accompanied by live music.

Diegetic, Nondiegetic, and Metadiegetic

A number of theorists discuss three types of music in terms of where it emanates (e.g., Bordwell and Thompson 2010; Gorbman 1987). First is **diegetic**: music that comes from within the

Figure 6.1 Georges Méliès (1861–1938) and Edwin S. Porter (1870–1941) and stills from their well-known silent films, *A Trip to the Moon* (1902) and *The Great Train Robbery* (1903), respectively

scene. Viewers see the orchestra, band, radio, MP3 player, or some other on-screen source of music. The second is **nondiegetic**: music that comes from an unknown source, such as music for background mood, a scene transition, or a thematic **leitmotif**—a melody specific to a character, setting, or similar story element. The third type is **metadiegetic**: music that is at first diegetic but later heard nondiegetically, or vice versa. For example, a juke box plays a love song in a diner when two lovers meet, and later the same song plays off screen when they come together again. In *Blazing Saddles* (Brooks 1974), Sheriff Bart (Cleavon Little) rides away accompanied by some nondiegetic swing jazz, but soon he rides by the Count Basie orchestra, out in the middle of a western no man's land, playing the music diegetically.

Parallel and Counterpoint

London (1936) was one of the first theorists to posit that music should **parallel** a scene's action. The melody, harmony, tempo, and instrumentation should correspond to the screen images in rhythm, form, tone, and movement. For example, fast action requires fast-paced, up-tempo music; sad scenes are heightened with slow-paced music—perhaps with the melancholic sound of a cello; noble characters are accompanied by regal sounds—such as those of trumpets; frightening moments are heightened by suspenseful music; and so on. Skiles (1976) reinforces this notion, listing what instruments best accompany different film and television genres: violins for romance, bassoon for humor, moog synthesizer for horror, and so on. Though London and Skiles wrote their arguments in the era of sound movies, film composers subscribed to this notion of parallel music since the beginning of cinema decades earlier. During the silent era, composers scored sheet music to be played live with films in the theaters where they screened. In the sound era, composers not only wrote but also recorded music to be mixed with movies' soundtracks—an art that continues today.

Eisenstein (1942, 1949) was the first to argue against parallelism in film music. He and his colleagues asserted the opposite—that music should stand in **counterpoint** to the images. For example, epic scenes should not be accompanied by epic scores, Hollywood style, but by minimalistic music that suggests the opposite of what is on the screen, Marxist style. In the Marxist tradition, this contrapuntal music enhances the **dialectic conflict** of the story. By seeing an image that suggests one type of feeling (thesis), while simultaneously hearing music that suggests a different feeling (antithesis), the viewers are required to work intellectually to reconcile the two feelings (synthesis). Eisenstein and others believe this engagement of the audience has greater value than having entertainment passively wash over the viewers, as is the case with parallel music that reinforces, rather than opposes, the images.

In our example script, *La Llorona*, parallel music is suggested for certain moments, such as frightening, frenetic music when Guadalupe drowns her babies and haunting, spiritual music when she wanders the earth. This music is only suggested because, in the end, the composer, not the screenwriter, chooses the music with the approval of the director. The composer might well decide to use some contrapuntal music, such as a happy tune when Guadalupe arrives at the river, rather than a foreboding melody, to contrast with the horrific deed she is about to do.

Three more examples illustrate the effective use of music. In *Psycho* (Hitchcock 1960), Bernard Hermann paralleled the famous stabbing scene in the shower with a bow screeching across violin strings. In *The Return of Martin Guerre* (Vigne 1982), set in France in the Late Middle Ages, the musical score is composed in the style of the time and played on medieval instruments, contributing to the authenticity of the setting. In *Amadeus* (Forman 1984), music is part of the story. In a pivotal scene, Mozart's wife brings to the jealous rival composer, Salieri, some sheets of original music that Mozart has composed. Salieri sees no crossed-out notes or erasures, realizing that Mozart is so gifted, he hears music in his head and simply jots the notes down. Salieri struggles with every composition; Mozart merely takes dictation. As Salieri stares at the pages, he hears in his head the beautiful music on those pages, becoming so overwhelmed that he lets the sheets drop to the floor. At this moment, the music drives the plot. Realizing that Mozart is the superior composer, Salieri turns on God, blaming God for breaking a covenant that Salieri believes they had—Salieri's chastity in exchange for God making him the greatest composer in the land. At that musical story beat, Salieri begins to plan his revenge against God by destroying God's creature, Mozart.

Sound Effects

The soundtrack of a drama also incorporates **sound effects** and any other aural elements that are created live or recorded, processed, edited, and mixed. Sound effects, like music, can both enhance a scene by their presence and drive the story. How many times have you watched a movie, TV show, or play in which a gunshot jolts a character into action? The gunshot startles the viewers, enhancing the scene and drawing them in, and it serves the story by setting up the next comic or dramatic moment.

Foley artists, named after the legendary Warner Bros. sound artist, Jack Foley, who raised movie sound effects to a new level, create the sounds for a scene by watching it on a screen and matching actions with appropriate noises. For example, they might punch a turkey for the fist sounds in a fight scene, or crinkle plastic wrap for a crackling fire, or step up and down in stilettos on a cobblestone patch on the floor to accompany the image of an actress walking in high heels on an old road. For other noises, recordists go on location to acquire "actual" sound elements, such as a metal rod striking a metal guide wire on a utility pole to create the sound of a laser shot. Other sounds are taken from prerecorded sound libraries, such as a variety of people laughing, horses trotting, tires screeching, and so on. The art of creating, recording, and mixing sound effects is a specialized field in production today, just like music composition, performance, recording, editing, and mixing.

The sound effects in *La Llorona* add atmosphere and move the story. The sad sound of the wind represents the cries of Guadalupe searching the earth. The sound of villagers mumbling in agreement with the old hag demonstrates society's disapproval of her illegitimate children. The sound of babies crying lets the viewers know on a literal level that babies are in the basket. On a metaphoric level, those cries represent the agony of the innocent who are sacrificed for others, as well as the agony that haunts those who kill them. The script allows a variety of other sound effects, too, such as night sounds (e.g., crickets, owls) for the opening and closing scenes, the exterior sounds of water rushing and wind rustling for the river scene, and so on.

Voice

Voice recording, editing, and mixing is also a specialized field. A sound team records dialogue as it happens, both on studio sets and on location. Often, a piece of dialogue is unusable because of some background noise (e.g., an airplane flying overhead), or the actors turn away from the mic during the scene, or the visual image is just right but the line reading is off, or some other problem arises. When this happens and there is no other take to use, the actors report to a sound stage where they watch the scene and record the needed lines of dialogue again. This is called **automated (or automatic) dialogue replacement (ADR)**, also known as **looping**. ADR is to voice what Foley is to sound effects: recording after the fact to correct mistakes or add to the soundtrack.

The dialogue in *La Llorona* is sparse, allowing the visuals to convey much of the story. Where it exists, the way the voices sound—their **timbre**—is a consideration. For example, the child is young enough to be innocent, so the child's voice should not be too mature.

The parent's character is loving, so the voice should be soothing rather than harsh. Guadalupe has no dialogue, but if the script were to be expanded to include dialogue for her, given what you know about her character, what kind of quality do you think her voice should have?

A few more examples. In the television show *Will & Grace* (1998–2006), one of the supporting characters, Karen Walker (Megan Mullally), had a particularly nasal, whispery, whining voice, in keeping with her annoying character. In *Star Wars* (Lucas 1977), who can forget the deep echo of Darth Vader's voice (James Earl Jones)? In animation, a wide range of character voices are heard, including bad guys with accents, much to the regret of many non-native citizens and immigrants.

These three categories of sound—music, sound effects, voice—comprise the bulk of sound theory. Mixing all three elements at appropriate moments on the soundtrack creates aural depth, bringing atmosphere to the drama. This, in turn, attracts viewers and engages them in the story more deeply than if the soundtrack were flat with just one aural element throughout, such as dialogue only. Many authors discuss in detail the element of sound (e.g., Alten 2005; Walters 1994; Zettl 2013).

To be sure, there are moments when a single audio element can be effective by its very isolation from other sounds, such as a scream amidst total silence. The choice for *no* music or *no* sound effects is sometimes the best choice. For example, in *La Llorona*, at the moment Guadalupe finishes pounding the cross into the ground, an eerie silence might be effective for a beat or two before the haunting sounds of murdered babies in the afterlife begin to chase her soul. Then again, maybe the haunting sounds should begin on the last hit of the rock against the cross.

Two more examples illustrate effective moments with minimal sound. The film *Rob Roy* (Caton-Jones 1995) features a sword fight at its climax. While many movie sword fights are accompanied by heart-racing music, in this case no music is heard. Instead, only the very real sounds of clashing metal and grunting, panting men carry the scene. These sounds convey the exhaustion of the protagonist and antagonist as they duel to the death. Music would be superfluous.

Conversely, music rather than sound effects effectively carries a montage sequence in *Good Morning, Vietnam* (Levinson 1987). We hear Louis Armstrong singing *What a Wonderful World* as we watch napalm being dropped and people fleeing for their lives. Rather than hearing the frightening sounds of war that could accompany the images, the happy lyrics of the song—an example of counterpoint music that seems the opposite of what the images suggest—cause the viewers to feel a level of uneasiness that is arguably greater than they would feel if they heard parallel battle sound effects.

Summary

While Aristotle discusses only **music** in his *Poetics* (*c*. 335 BCE), two additional aural elements are significant in sound theory today: **sound effects** and **voice**. Each of these three categories of sound is a specialty in the world of production because each has such great potential to contribute to the overall drama when handled effectively, or to distract from the drama when handled poorly. Screenwriters should *not overwrite* the aural elements of a script, leaving the details to the **production team** instead. However, when a certain piece or type of music, sound effect, or vocal element is necessary to the story or to a character, the screenwriter should be familiar with these categories of sound so he or she can write appropriate aural description and action.

Music sets mood, as does the purposive lack of music in select places. Music can also **reveal character** (e.g., a protagonist's **leitmotif**) and **advance story** (e.g., a music cue that leads to a character's subsequent action). The source of music may appear on the screen **diegetically**, or it may be off screen **nondiegetically**, or it may be a mix of both **metadiegetically**. Music may **parallel** the action of the story, or it may stand in **counterpoint** to the image on the screen or stage. **Sound effects** add audio depth to the soundtrack, making the audience feel more **present** in the scene. Sound effects can also **advance plot** (e.g., a gunshot) and **reveal character** (e.g., the tick of a well-dressed man's pocket watch). **Voice** characteristics can also be important to *character* (e.g., accents from different countries) and to **story advancement** (e.g., a person's cry in one scene carries over into the next scene).

Reflection and Discussion

1. In the previous "Reflection and Discussion" exercises, you developed a scene that embodies a major theme from your life. What elements of music, sound effects, and voice, can you add to this scene to enhance that life lesson without overwriting too much detail that the production team should be left to handle?
2. Look up the Academy Awards, or Oscars, for the most recent year. What film received the Oscar for Sound Editing and for Sound Mixing? Watch these films (or one film if a single film won both categories). What do you notice about the soundtrack of this film or these films that made it sufficiently outstanding to receive an Oscar?
3. Now look up the most recent Oscar recipients for Music—Original Score and Music—Original Song. Watch these films. What do you notice about the score and song that you think made them Oscar-worthy?

7

Spectacle

The sixth and final of Aristotle's elements is **spectacle**. Additional translations of the Greek *opsis* include "apparatus," "mise-en-scène," "opticals," "plastics," and "visuals." Spectacle incorporates all the visual elements of drama. It is "what the play looks like."

Spectacle for Screenwriters

Why include a chapter on spectacle in this primer about story structure? Screenwriters must know all the elements that comprise the art form for which they are writing: motion image with sound. All the elements that comprise spectacle can reveal location, time, style, and character. Spectacle can also advance the story and point to theme. For this reason, writers must know the basics of these elements to incorporate them effectively in their stories.

Spectacle includes everything the viewers see: **locations** and **sets**, **lighting** and **shadow**, **wardrobe** or **costumes**, **hair** and **makeup**, and **properties**. **Actors' physical features**, as well as *gestures* and *movement*, are also incorporated in this category. Additionally, just as sound can be recorded, processed, edited, and mixed, so can visual elements. Spectacle therefore includes **camera shots** and **movement**, as well as **special visual effects** and **editing**. Many scholars expand on the aesthetics of spectacle and/or the theories and techniques of shooting and editing (e.g., Boggs and Petrie 2011; Burdick 1974; Compesi 2006; Foust, Fink, and Gross 2012; Gross 2009; Katz 1992; Mamer 2008; Millerson 2012; Musburger 2010; Owens and Millerson 2011; Parker, Wolf, and Block 2008; Richards 1992; Roth 1983; Salvaggio 1980; Zettl 2011).

The spectacle of drama underscores and reinforces the other elements. Additionally, like all elements of drama, spectacle attracts and holds viewers. The look of the story may be realistic or abstract. It may be lavish or minimal. It may be what the viewers expect, or it may surprise them. The art director imagines and the design team creates the look of a drama with sets, lights, wardrobe, hair-makeup, props, and actors' physical features. The creation of the visuals enhances the meaning of each moment in the story while keeping the audience focused on that moment.

Our sample script, *La Llorona*, lends itself to a number of different visual interpretations. The bookend scenes with the child and parent could take place in a realistic nighttime bedroom, or somewhere more abstract to signify the human quest for myth and legend. Guadalupe's village could be revealed in daylight—signifying that her sin is open for all to see and condemn—or at night—signifying the darkness that surrounds her and the others. The drowning could be shown from a variety of abnormal camera angles to heighten the horror. The image of Guadalupe's soul roaming the earth suggests a more surrealistic, less realistic mix of light, color, setting, costume, makeup, and camera angle. In the end, it is the director's duty and privilege to interpret the script and to communicate his or her vision to the art director, cinematographer-videographer, and all the designers, who in turn create the look, or spectacle, of the drama.

That noted, screen authors should *not overwrite* the visual elements of their stories. The director has the final say regarding a film's look. The art director is responsible for unifying the visual elements of a production. The art director works with the cinematographer or director of photography (DP) and all the design team—location scout, sets, lights, costumes, hair-makeup, and props—to achieve the production's look. The casting director selects the actors (except the principals, who are usually cast by the director), and the physical features of those actors are one of many considerations in casting. For these reasons, a screenwriter should *not* describe every detail of a costume or furniture or properties. These details are determined by others.

However, when a particular visual element is necessary to the story or to a character, then and only then should the writer include that in the screenplay. For example, in *La Llorona*, it is important to write in the script that Guadalupe drowns her twin infants in a river because that is part of the legend. In any science fiction movie or television series (e.g., the *Star Trek* franchise of multiple movies and TV shows), enough visual elements must be written to convey the idea of characters or creatures from another world and locations that do not exist when scenes occur somewhere beyond our known world. In *Zero Dark Thirty* (Bigelow 2012), writer Mark Boal had to include enough visual description to capture what the manhunt for Osama bin Laden might have looked like, without burdening the script with unnecessary details that the art director, cinematographer, and design team created. For example, it is important to note when a scene occurs on a crowded street in Abbottabad, Pakistan, but it would be only clutter to write that "hundreds of extras dressed in Islamic clothing, including women in burkas, mill about." Those extras and burkas and milling about are assumed in "a crowded street in Abbottabad," so the production team researches, fleshes out, and creates those details.

Locations and Sets

The setting of a screenplay can be anywhere, limited only by the writer's imagination. It is useful for writers, as well as all involved in

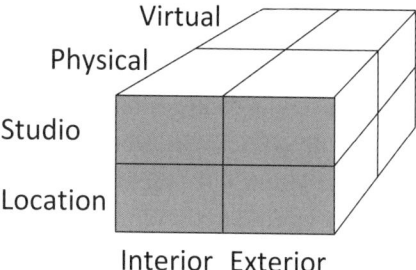

Figure 7.1 A model of three dimensions to consider regarding scene settings: interior or exterior, location or studio (stage or lot), and physical or virtual (or combination)

making movies and television, to consider settings on at least three dimensions: location or studio (stage or back lot), interior or exterior, and physical or virtual. Figure 7.1 illustrates this.

Location or Studio

The setting of a scene can be either a **location**—a place away from a **studio**—or it can be a **set** created in a studio **sound stage** or on a **back lot**. Screenwriters do not write in the script if a scene occurs on location or on a lot; however, it is important to know the possibilities when penning a screenplay. The important thing for the writer is to set scenes wherever they best serve the story. For example, *The Da Vinci Code* (Howard 2006) and its sequel *Angels & Demons* (Howard 2009) necessarily require locations and sets in Rome and Vatican City. The budget and the producing and directing teams, not the writing teams, determine what shots, if any, are actually in Rome (e.g., wide shots of the city skyline, though those can be stock video or still shots), what shots are in a city doubling as Rome (tighter shots with enough background to establish location), what shots are on streets built on a studio back lot to look like Rome, and what shots are on sets built on sound stages.

Interior or Exterior

All locations and sets are considered to be either "interior" or "exterior." In fact, every new scene in a screenplay or teleplay begins with a **slug line** that starts with one of two abbreviations, either "INT." or "EXT."—always capitalized (see Chapter 10). That abbreviation is followed by a one- or two-word description of the space, such as "INT. JOES' APARTMENT," or "EXT. MEADOW"—still in ALL CAPS. For the screenwriter, making those creative choices for the story is critical. Where should each scene be located to say the most about the characters at that moment and to advance the story? The design team, and not the writer, then decides how best to create that setting: location or studio, actual or constructed.

Physical or Virtual

Sets and locations can also be *physical*—actually constructed sets or places—or they can be *virtual*—**computer-generated imagery (CGI)** created in a computer—or they can be **CGI-enhanced**—a combination of both a physical set or location with CGI elements added (e.g., photographed vistas of New Zealand with CGI elements added to create Middle Earth in Peter Jackson's films adapted from the writings of J.R.R. Tolkien). For virtual sets, the actors typically perform in front of, or surrounded by, a **green screen** (it can also be blue or, really, any color, but green is the most-used because it is the farthest primary color away from skin color on the color spectrum—skin has more red and even a little blue because of arteries and veins). After the scene is recorded, a computer removes the green and replaces it with the set or exterior location that has been photographed and imported into the computer or that has been generated within the computer itself.

Realistic or Nonrealistic

The look of a set can be anywhere on the continuum from realistic to nonrealistic (see Chapter 8, 8.3). A very realistic set might be **naturalistic**—an actual construction of a complete room or location, say, a bathroom with a real working sink, toilet, and shower that an actor can use during a scene. If that same bathroom has a sink, toilet, and shower that appear real on camera, but don't actually function, that is still a **realistic** set, though not fully naturalistic. Now let's say our character has a dream that occurs in a bathroom. Dreams are not realistic, so the sink, toilet, and shower might be represented by geometric shapes rather than by the actual fixtures. Those shapes are more **symbolic** than realistic. Then our character plunges into a psychotic abyss in which the real world is completely out of whack. The set designer might create even more distorted images that do not even look like bathroom fixtures, creating a completely **abstract** set. That set can be physical or CGI, as well as interior or exterior.

For the screenwriter, it is important to know the many possibilities of locations and sets; however, these details do not belong in screenplays. The writer's job is to select or imagine a location for each scene that best fits the story at that moment. It is the director's and design team's job to work out the details—not only for locations and sets but for all the elements of spectacle discussed here.

Lights and Shadow

All lighting is considered to be "day" or "night." To be sure, scenes take place at dawn and dusk, as well, but typically a scene is designated as either day or night. In fact, every slug line ends with a hyphen followed by either the word "day" or "night," such as "INT. JOE'S APARTMENT—NIGHT" or "EXT. MEADOW—DAY." The lighting director then makes the necessary tweaks depending on the precise time of day or night, including dawn, morning, high noon, afternoon, evening, or dusk. Lighting for day is also called **high-key lighting**, meaning generally bright illumination overall with little **shadow**. Lighting for night is also called **low-key lighting**, meaning generally dark overall, with many shadows, but still enough light to see a face or painting or whatever needs to be visible.

As with sets, lighting varies depending on whether the scene is interior or exterior. Interior scenes are obviously shot mostly indoor with indoor lighting instruments (either up on a studio grid or on stands on the floor), and exterior scenes are shot mostly outdoors with sunlight and reflectors or sun-balanced lights to reduce shadow (if daytime). However, variations occur. The earliest film studios, such as Edison's Black Maria (see Figure 7.2), had walls, but the roof was open to let in sunlight—something like a partially exterior space to shoot interior scenes. Likewise, sound stages can house exterior sets, with streets and gardens and fields moving off to a horizon line, possibly

Figure 7.2 Thomas Edison (1847–1931) and filmmaker William Dickson (1860–1935), with their "Black Maria" studio, an early film stage of the Edison Company in New Jersey, which was built on a circular track to rotate with the sun during the day

ending at a painted continuation of that same street or garden or field (e.g., *The Wizard of Oz*, Fleming 1939), or maybe ending in a scrim with, say, blue lighting and cloud patterns to represent the sky (*Dracula*, Coppola 1992). In these cases, exteriors are actually shot indoors, allowing for greater control of lighting and sound than on location.

Like sets, lighting can also be realistic or nonrealistic. Realistic lighting causes people and objects to appear the way we normally perceive them in our world, usually achieved by the **three-point lighting** scheme that includes a key, back, and fill light, as discussed in any photography, film, or video production textbook, or online. Nonrealistic lighting can include everything from the sharp contrast of bright and dark found in **expressionism** (e.g., *Nosferatu,* Murnau 1922) to the **cinéma vérité** or observational style of **impressionism** (e.g., *Sausalito*, Stauffacher 1948, with influences in films such as Kubrick's *The Shining* 1980) to the saturated colors and images of dreams that are **surrealism** (e.g., the dancing Hefalumps and Woozels in *Winnie the Pooh and the Blustery Day*, Reitherman 1968). Even in animated and CGI films, lighting is a principal consideration. Though no physical lighting instruments are required, a lighting director still gives direction, shape, intensity, shadow, color, and texture to the animated or computer-generated lighting.

Costume and Wardrobe

The **costume designer** and **wardrobe** department interpret the screenplay and acquire or create the clothing for the actors. One consideration is the time period of the story: past, present, or future. If the past, the designer researches the era to determine wardrobe. If the present, the designer works with today's fashions. If the future, the designer is freed from considerations of what has been or what is now to create something unknown. That unknown wardrobe might reflect past and present designs, or it might be something altogether fantastical.

Another consideration is how realistic or nonrealistic the costumes should be. In a **costume drama**—a period piece set in an earlier time period—the wardrobe should look as if it could realistically be in that era, though some heightened styling might occur to enhance spectacle. A contemporary drama or comedy should have costumes that reflect the current era, though again some heightened stylization might occur. For a futuristic film or TV series, if the intent is to present what could be a realistic look into the future, then a realistic, though also futuristic, wardrobe is called for. If the future is presented in a more abstract manner, then less realistic and more abstract costumes are called for.

Figure 7.3 Medieval drawings of different classes wearing different clothing

Yet another consideration in outfitting actors with wardrobe is each character's place in society. In a medieval setting, the upper class would dress in fine costumes worthy of their nobility, while the lower class would dress in simple shirts and pants, even rags, to reflect their status (see Figure 7.3). In a contemporary piece, most people in most classes could wear clothing within a normal range, from jeans to suits; still, a costumer might make some class distinctions, such as a wealthier boss wearing a tailored suit made of fine wool while his less wealthy subordinate wears less well-fitting clothes off the rack. In *Erin Brockovich* (Soderbergh 2000), the title character (Julia Roberts) dresses like an unemployed single mom, while the lawyers for the power company dress like powerful attorneys.

Hair and Makeup

As with wardrobe, the **hair** and **makeup** department interprets a script to determine its setting of time and location, whether real or fantasy, and the status of the characters in that world. For example, the hair and makeup of the players in *Les Misérables* (novel, Hugo 1862; stage musical, 1985; film musical, Hooper 2012), should represent French characters in the early 1800s. Those with power, such as Javert (Russell Crowe in the 2012 film), appear more aristocratic than those without power, such as Jean Valjean (Hugh Jackman) when he escapes from prison, though his hair and makeup change as he works his way up the social ladder to power. The disempowered, such as Fantine (Anne Hathaway) and her illegitimate daughter Cosette (Amanda Seyfried) have less-arranged hair and makeup to reinforce their lower-class status (see Figure 7.4). When the "real" world (quotation marks because this is a sung-through musical, so the world is not realistic, but it does represent a very heightened version of the "actual" world of nineteenth-century France) gives way to the spirit world at the end, much more fanciful hair and makeup are called for.

Figure 7.4 Victor Hugo (1802–1885) and an illustration of Cosette sweeping from the first publication of *Les Misérables* (1862)

Makeup typically enhances an actor's features, covering up blemishes and correcting defects to make the actor appear real on screen without the audience being distracted by the usual imperfections we all have (e.g., acne, bags under eyes, crow's feet). In the art of **special effects' makeup,** the actor's features are completely transformed to create a new creature. The makeup can be physical (e.g., F. Murray Abraham's transformation as old Salieri in *Amadeus*, Forman 1984), or it can be CGI (e.g., Bill Nighy's transformation as the squid-bearded Davy Jones in *Pirates of the Caribbean: Dead Man's Chest*, Verbinski 2006). As with sets, lights, and wardrobe, even when characters are created within computers, hair and makeup artists are important in determining their appearance. These artists bring their expertise to bear on the CGI people. Examples include the blue, three-meter tall Na'vi of Pandora in James Cameron's *Avatar* (2009) and the troll-like inhabitants of Middle Earth in Peter Jackson's *The Lord of the Rings* and *The Hobbit* trilogies. For a writer, the key is to remember is that hair and makeup artists can create anything, real or imaginary, so let your imagination run wild.

Properties

Properties, or **props**, are also purchased and created to reflect the setting of each story in time and place, whether realistic or not, and the socio-economic status of the characters who use those props. As with all the elements of spectacle, props can be physical or CGI. Examples of physical props can be seen in any pre-CGI film because there was no way to create them in computers and add them to a screen, such as the Maltese Falcon statuette in the film of the same name (Huston 1941). Examples of CGI props can be seen in computer-animated films, such as Woody's holster or Buzz's flip-out wings in the *Toy Story* franchise (Pixar). In some cases, props might be a bit of both, such as the light sabers in *Star Wars* (Lucas 1977) that are physical props in the actors' hands with light beams added optically (optical effects preceded CGI effects). For writers, again, imagination is the key regarding props, knowing that prop masters can find, make, or use a computer to create anything.

Actors' Physical Features

Another element of spectacle consists of the **physical features** of the actors themselves or other on-camera **talent**—anyone who appears on camera, whether as himself or herself or acting the role of another. To be sure, hair and makeup, costume, and props can alter those features, sometimes a lot (Jim Carrey in *How the Grinch Stole Christmas*, Howard 2000), or somewhat (Daniel Day-Lewis in *Lincoln*, Spielberg 2012), or less but still transforming (Meryl Streep as Margaret Thatcher in *The Iron Lady*, Lloyd 2011, or as Julia Childs in *Julie & Julia*, Ephron 2009), or little to none (Halle Barry in *Monster's Ball*,

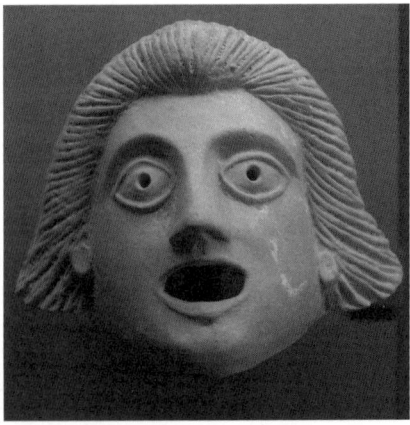

Figure 7.5 Theater mask of a youth from the 1st century BCE

Forster 2001). Whether heavily made up or not, the actor's appearance is part of the spectacle of drama.

In ancient Greek and Roman theater, actors wore masks as part of the spectacle (see Figure 7.5). Each mask was designed to convey an emotion, and by seeing the masks, the viewers could interpret the emotion of each character's words and actions at any point in the play. The masks also had a more utilitarian function: folks in the back could see what was going on. For example, masks with horrified looks on the chorus would convey their fright as they see Oedipus emerge from the palace with his eyes gouged out.

Blocking and Camera Shots

While the director decides the blocking and camera shots for stage and screen, the writer should know the basic language of these considerations for use in his or her scripts. As with other elements of spectacle, it is important not to overwrite description. However, where a particular movement or shot is necessary for a character or story beat, that note should be included in the script.

Blocking refers to the movement and arrangement of the actors on a set, along with the placement of the cameras for film and television. On stage, actors' movements are referenced from their point of view; that is, "stage right" means the actor's right, and "stage left" means the actor's left. On screen, the directions are reversed, with "screen right" being the audience's right or actor's left (assuming the actor is facing the camera), and "screen left" being the audience's left or actor's right. On both stage and screen, "up stage" refers to the direction of the stage away from the audience or camera, while "down stage" refers to the stage area closes to audience and camera.

Camera **shots** have different meanings (see Chapter 2). A **long shot** (LS) or **wide shot** (WS) means a broad vista that shows the environment and full actors' bodies. It is used to establish a scene. A **medium shot** (MS) generally reveals an actor from about the waist up. It is used to bring the viewers closer to the action and dialogue. A *close-up* is usually a head-and-shoulders shot. It is the strongest shot psychologically and is used to intensify emotion as well as to reveal small items and gestures on the screen (e.g., a watch, the wink of an eye). Different directors use these terms to frame shots slightly differently. For writers, it is useful to know generally what they mean. In many scripts, the phrase **ANGLE ON** is used to note when the camera needs to show something of note, such as "ANGLE ON clock" to show the time. Again, the director chooses the specific length of that angle.

Likewise, the terms for camera movement can be useful if necessary for the story, but not superfluous—again, the director ultimately makes decisions about camera perspectives. A **dolly shot** moves the camera closer to (dolly in) or away from (dolly back) from the actors. This has the visual effect of moving the audience toward or away from the scene. This is different from a **zoom-in** or **zoom-out**, which manipulates the lens to magnify or de-magnify the image and has the visual effect of moving the scene closer to or farther away from the audience. A **tracking shot** moves the camera laterally relative to the actors, primarily left and right. This term comes from the practice of laying down tracks to move a camera smoothly over rough terrain. It has the effect of moving the audience along with the actors. This is different from a **panning shot**, which keeps the camera stationary but pivots the head left or right and has the effect of turning the audience's head. A **crane** or **boom shot** moves the camera high overhead. It has the effect of raising the audience to a higher story. This is different from a **pedestal shot**, where the camera remains on the ground but the pedestal mechanism raises or lowers. This has the effect of the viewer standing or squatting.

Most scenes are shot in the **third person**, which means the actors remain objective relative to the camera: "he," "she," and "they." If the camera takes on the viewpoint of a character within the story, perhaps cutting away to something a character sees, that is the **first person** camera perspective, "I," also called a **point of view** or simply **POV** shot in which the camera becomes the eyes of a character. Some scripts indicate a POV shot, such as "JANE'S POV," if that is important at that moment in the story. If the actors look right into the camera, that is the **second person** perspective, or "you," also called **direct address** because they directly address the audience through the lens, or **reportorial** because news reporters use this perspective when delivering the news.

For this direct-address shot, the actor breaks the **fourth wall**. Normally, actors play a scene as if in their own world, say, an interior with three visible walls (back and two side walls) while the camera "looks in" as if through an invisible fourth wall. When an actor looks into the lens, he or she looks through, or breaks, that invisible wall.

Special Effects

The area of **special visual effects** has always been important in film, from the early days to today, from Georges Méliès' *A Trip to the Moon* (1902) to the fantastical effects of Buster Keaton to the thrill of the original *King Kong* (1933) to the burning of Atlanta in *Gone with the Wind* (Fleming 1939) to the swirling tornado and Glinda's ball in

The Wizard of Oz (Fleming 1939) all the way to the sinking of the *Titanic* (Cameron 1997) and the end of the world in *2012*, (Emmerich 2009). Before the modern era of computer-generated effects, specialists relied on models, rear-screen projection, camera angles, stop-motion photography, optical processing, and other mechanical tricks for effects. Even in today's digital world, some directors and visual effects' artists prefer physical to CGI effects, such as real explosions, actual fake blood, and so on. They like the look of the "real" effect rather than the "computer" effect. Some directors use both. For example, James Cameron built a scale mock-up of the ship Titanic for some of the scenes in that film (1997), but he also used a good deal of CGI and CGI-enhanced imagery, rendering together the physical and computer effects seamlessly into a masterpiece with stunning spectacle.

Editing

Like all the other areas of spectacle, **editing** is handled by trained specialists. Also like other areas, screenwriters should know the basic vocabulary to include editing descriptions in their screenplays if appropriate, but only sparsely, never overwriting, including just what needs to be said for story and character. When editing a transition from one camera shot to another, the straight **cut** is the most-used transition. This signifies that the shots belong *together in time and place*. Think of a simple dialogue scene that cuts back and forth between the characters as they speak. The **dissolve** is a slow blending of scenes as one transforms into the other over a period of seconds. This signifies a *change in time and place*. It can also be used effectively in a slow **montage** sequence of images. The **wipe** is a geometric pattern that replaces one shot with another, such as a diamond shape replacing a shot of a baseball diamond (get it?) with a playback shot. This draws attention to the transition itself, signifying a *major change* between the two images. A **key** or **superimposition (super)** places one image into or over another, such as a reporter's name on the **lower-third** of the television screen during a news feature. (Technically, a "key" replaces just the part of the first image with the desired part of the second image, such as the letters of a person's name, something like a stencil or cookie-cutter into the image, while a "superimposition" layers one entire image over the other, rather than just selected parts or pixels, in a "half dissolve.")

For writers, it is rarely necessary to write "cut to" because the cut is the assumed transition. Sometimes a writer will note a **smash cut** to signal a rapid cut for effect, such as when a character says, "John will never go for that," followed by a smash cut to John saying, "Sure, I'll go for that." A writer might write "dissolve to" or "wipe to" to signal the use of one of these transition types that moves the audience across time or space; however, the director ultimately makes the decisions regarding scene transitions, so writing these transitions is often superfluous. Use with caution, and then only when necessary. Many others offer greater detail about editing theory and practice (e.g., Bazin 1967; Eisenstein 1942; Zettl 2013).

It should be noted that the elements of spectacle discussed here combine as a whole to create a play's **mise-en-scène**, literally "meaning of the scene." While each is examined here separately for the sake of analysis, they all work together to create the look of a drama (comic or serious)—its overall visual style. Additional examples illustrate this. *The Cabinet of Dr Caligari* (Wiene 1920) utilizes nonrealistic sets, heavy lighting contrast (bright against dark), exaggerated costuming, hair and makeup, all to establish its expressionistic style. In contrast, *Saving Private Ryan* (Spielberg 1998) uses realistic sets and lighting, with many actual locations and realistic uniforms from World War II, along with hair and makeup in the style of that period, all to convey the film's all-too-real, naturalistic style. Some productions combine different styles when appropriate. For example, most productions of *A Christmas Carol* (Dickens 1843) move between a semi-realistic visual style for Scrooge's Dickensian world and a dream-like surrealistic style for Scrooge's encounters with the three ghosts of Christmases Past, Present, and Future. Westerns have a brownish, sepia tone to the colors, suggesting the look of older film to correspond with the older time, along with sets and locations and costumes that together signify the style of the old west. Children's television programs use bright lights and primary colors: colors that children learn early at home or in preschool and that reinforce the happy themes of the shows. Fantasy films rely heavily on CGI to create worlds that do not actually exist.

Summary

Knowing the elements that comprise a story's *spectacle* is important to writers. They should describe the *visual aspects* of scenes that are important for **character** and **story without overwriting** details that are the purview of the *director* and others to determine. Spectacle consists of all the elements that are seen: the *visuals*. These include the **locations** and **sets**, **lighting** and **shadows**, **costumes** and **wardrobe**, **hair** and **makeup**, **properties**, **actors' physical features**, **blocking** and **camera shots**, **special effects**, and **editing**. Artists in each of these areas are hired for productions, whether their creations are *physical* or *virtual*—**computer-generated imagery** (CGI). Their expertise brings each of these areas of spectacle to life to tell each story effectively. The *writer* creates and imagines the settings; the *director* interprets them; the *design team* makes them. Together, all the elements of spectacle create the visual meaning of a scene—its **mise-en-scène**.

Reflection and Discussion

1. So far in the "Reflection and Discussion" exercises, you have thought of a plot and developed characters that point to an important theme in your life, and you have created dialogue and sound for your scene. Now imagine the best and most appropriate spectacle for that scene, and write it with only brief but necessary descriptions of those visual elements. Be sure not to overwrite details that others work out, but write

just what is important in the setting that reveals character and advances your story.
2. Think of some of your favorite movie images. Perhaps they include Charlie Chaplin twisting through the giant cogs of a gear in *Modern Times* (Chaplin 1936), or Slim Pickens riding an atom bomb as it drops at the end of *Dr Strangelove* (Kubrick 1964), or a giant T-Rex attacking innocent children in *Jurassic Park* (Spielberg 1993), or the spectacle of *Pan's Labyrinth* (del Toro 2006). Now consider why your favorite images might be so memorable to you. Was it the genius of the work (*Modern Times*), or an "I've never seen that before" moment (*Dr Strangelove*), or an image that elicited strong emotion (e.g., fear in *Jurassic Park*), or just the sheer beauty of it all (*Pan's Labyrinth*)? These examples are just to get you started. What other examples and reasons for their being memorable come to your mind?
3. Attend a local stage play in your community. Observe all the elements of spectacle: sets, lights, costumes, hair, makeup, props, actors' appearances, and any effects. Why do you think each designer (set, lights, costumes, etc.) made the choices he or she made in interpreting the play? Do you think those choices enhanced or hindered the script? Why?

8

Unity, Metaphor, Universality, Catharsis, and Style

In addition to Aristotle's six elements, at least five other important concepts arise from an analysis of the literature of dramatic theory: **unity**, **metaphor**, **style**, **universality**, and **catharsis**. As with the elements discussed in the other chapters, these additional five concepts are vital in understanding drama. That makes them vital to writers in creating drama, as well.

Unity

Conventional dramatic theory often includes discussion of the three **unities**: action, time, and place. Additionally, many scholars discuss the unity of theme, which remains relevant today. Each is discussed here in turn.

Unity of Action

Aristotle founded the idea of unity of action. In his discussion of plot, he observed that the action of a play should be one, singular whole, with each moment leading logically to the next. Today, of course, many plays have multiple plots, or A-, B-, and C-stories. Yet, in a well-structured play, even multiple storylines are unified in their themes (more later). The B- and C-stories reinforce the A-story in their principal ideas or lessons.

In our example script, *La Llorona*, there are two plots that comprise the **story-within-a-story** structure. In the **framing** story, which is the B-story, the bookend scenes in the contemporary world reveal a loving relationship between parent and child. This relationship reinforces the relationship between Guadalupe and her newborn twins in the primary story set in a past village, which is the A-story. Guadalupe loves her children or she would not mourn their loss throughout eternity. This love—reinforced in the B-story in the opening and closing scenes—sets up the horror of Guadalupe's murder by contrasting so starkly with her love. Or perhaps her love drives her to do the deed so her children are not forced to grow up in a society that condemns them because of the circumstance of their birth.

Another example is the venerable *Hamlet* (Shakespeare 1603) (see Chapter 5, Figure 5.2). The main plot—Hamlet's vengeance of his father's murder—is linked thematically with one of the subplots—Laertes's return from France to avenge his father's death. Unity of action, then, is a relevant dramatic concept today, even when a play has more than one plot: the different actions (stories) are unified in supporting the drama's theme.

Unity of Time and Place

The remaining two unities of time and place are historically significant, but no longer "requirements" for today's drama. Some scholars (e.g., Cooper 1923) note that these two ideas were developed in the sixteenth century and mistakenly attributed to the ancient Greeks. The unity of time refers to the observation that all the action of a drama occurs within one day. The unity of place means the action takes place in one location. Certainly a play may adhere to these principles, such as *Oedipus Rex* (Sophocles *c.* 429 BCE)—the drama on which Aristotle based his concepts. A personal favorite episode of the hit TV series *Mad About You* (1992–1999) featured one episode in real time in which all 22 minutes were performed without an edit as new parents Paul and Jamie Buchman (Paul Reiser and Helen Hunt, respectively) accidentally locked their child in the bathroom and waited anxiously outside while figuring out how to rescue her.

Exceptions such as these noted, many dramatic stories do not take place in real time or in one day. Particularly in television and film drama, plays often span more than one day with action taking place in many locations. In the example of *La Llorona*, the opening and closing scenes are in a contemporary child's bedroom, while the story of Guadalupe is told in settings that include a village in some bygone era, a river, some type of countryside through which her soul wanders, and maybe even other times and places that a dramatist might add if the script were to be embellished for a longer-form screenplay.

Another example is *The Godfather: Part II* (Coppola 1974), which covers about the first half of the twentieth century. Flashbacks to the young Don Corleone in the early 1900s are intercut with scenes of his son Michael in the mid-1900s. While the film takes place across multiple times and settings, the scenes—past and present—are all unified thematically. Each reveals some aspect of either father Don's or son Michael's rise to power in the mob world. With each step up the ladder to power, each loses a piece of his soul or conscience. At first, each commits minor crimes, such as theft. Each then moves to larger crimes, such as extortion. Ultimately, each commits the most heinous of crimes, murder.

Unity of Theme

A play for the screen (any size) or stage may have one A-story or multiple stories—B, C, maybe even more—depending on the play's length and complexity. A play may take place in real time or perhaps in a somewhat real-time day, or it may span weeks, months, years, centuries, or even millennia. A play may take place in one location, maybe with a few rooms or even an exterior porch or yard added, or it may take place across multiple settings, cities, countries, continents, or even planets. Whether a play adheres to the traditional unities of action, time, and place or not, a well-told story adheres to the **unity of theme**. If not, what is the point of multiple storylines or multiple time and location settings? Without unity of theme, a story would be disjointed and confusing.

Consider *The Taming of the Shrew* (Shakespeare 1590) (see Figure 8.1). Both the A- and B-stories find men pursuing the love of women—sisters, in fact. In the A-Story, Petruchio—a sly gentleman—attempts to woo Katherina, or Kate, the shrew. In the B-story, Lucentio, a star-crossed romantic, pursues Kate's sweet and lovely sister, Bianca, along with other suitors. The stories contrast in many ways, including the sisters' personalities and the men's different approaches to love; yet, in that contrast, Shakespeare explores the unified and eternal theme of the sometimes

Figure 8.1 A photo of Kate and Petruchio in Shakespeare's *The Taming of the Shrew* (c. 1592)

impossible and always problematic attraction of the sexes in a delightfully comic (albeit somewhat misogynistic) manner.

More currently, consider the film *Crash* (Haggis 2004). This drama features an ensemble cast of characters, each living in Los Angeles, each facing problems and crises in his or her life. Yet, all the stories intertwine, ultimately exploring the theme of racism. The specific thematic statement is that racism destroys, as evidenced by its destructive effect on all the characters' lives in the highly diverse city of LA.

Metaphor

An important technique that contributes to thematic unity is **metaphor**. Many theorists (e.g., Withers 1983) observe that metaphor is created when unrelated objects—both aural and visual—become related through juxtaposition. Hodge (1999) refers to metaphorical elements as "master images" for a production. Kitatani (1985) notes that metaphor enhances drama by creating underlying relationships between the formal elements of a play.

Metaphor can be developed creatively to manipulate viewers cognitively and affectively. *Cognitive* manipulation refers to viewers' thoughts, making them think something at a particular moment in a story, even if that "something" is not on screen but is only represented by a metaphoric element. *Affective* manipulation refers to viewers' emotions, making them feel something at a particular moment in the story through metaphoric association. This manipulation engages the audience and helps relate the story to the viewers (see "universality" in next section). Metaphor can make the audience think about, or feel for, a character or idea when that character is not in view or that idea is not expressly stated.

In *La Llorona*, a director might create several metaphors. For example, the child in the opening and closing scenes could have a toy in bed, and a similar toy could appear in the basket with the babies that Guadalupe carries, thereby unifying the child in the contemporary B-story with the children in the A-story of a bygone time. Among many possible other metaphors in the script, religious metaphors abound, specifically Christian metaphors. The children are like innocent lambs. Their cries could sound like sheep bleating. They are offered as a sacrifice to reconcile sinner and sin—their mother and her shame. The mother creates a makeshift cross (Jesus was crucified) to mark her babies' tomb, but the tomb is empty (Jesus was resurrected). The mother is doomed to eternal perdition, able to obtain eternal rest only when her soul is cleansed. She tries to earn that rest by looking for her babies' drowned bodies so she can bury them properly, but she is unsuccessful, just as many believers attempt to earn their own salvation and fail. In Christian theology, people do not and cannot save themselves by their own actions; only God saves through His forgiveness of sins that comes from His sacrifice of His child to pay the price for sin (Ephesians 2:8–9). Similarly, Guadalupe sacrifices her children to pay the price of her fornication, but she cannot herself earn eternal rest. Forgiveness from God is necessary for eternal peace, and that forgiveness is what Guadalupe's soul must experience.

In another example of effective metaphor, *The Glass Menagerie* (Williams 1945) features a collection of small glass animals (see Figure 8.2). This menagerie becomes a *symbol* for Laura's frailty through its association with her in the play. When one of the animals is broken, this action metaphorically shatters her fragile dreams. In *Doctor Zhivago* (Lean 1965), in every scene in which Lara (Julie Christie) appears—the title character's love interest—there are flowers, making flowers her metaphoric symbol. In one winter scene, Dr Zhivago (Omar Sharif) looks out the window, which is covered with ice crystals. Those crystals slowly dissolve into flowers, signifying the passing of time from winter to spring. When the viewers see those flowers, they think of Lara because flowers have become her metaphor. Through metaphor rather than dialogue, the audience knows that Dr Zhivago is thinking of Lara, even though she is not on the

Figure 8.2 Tennessee Williams (1911–1983) and a glass unicorn possibly of the type found in his play, *The Glass Menagerie* (1944), the menagerie serving as a metaphor for the fragile Laura Wingfield

screen at that moment, and we know he will return to her in the spring thaw. In *Star Wars* (Lucas 1977), each character has a musical theme, or melody, that serves as a **leitmotif** for that character. The leitmotif serves as an aural metaphor. When that leitmotif plays, the audience thinks of that character, whether or not that character appears on screen at that moment.

Universality

Universality refers to the relevance of a play to its audience. How effectively does the drama reach its viewers? How well does it address their lives?

Universality is attained through the symbiosis of all the elements of drama. For example, Aristotle (*c.* 335 BCE) argues that **plot** should imitate action that is necessary or probable (see Chapter 2). In other words, the story should be understandable to its audience. Many dramatists (e.g., Muller 1973) discuss the need for *characters* to be identifiable to the audience in order to attract viewer interest (see Chapter 3). Their **ethos** must elicit **pathos**, making the viewers care about them (see Chapter 3). Some theorists (e.g., Rosenthal 1973) cite the need for a play's **theme** to be timely in the viewers' lives (see Chapter 4). The moral point must be relevant to the audience. What themes are relevant? Some authors (e.g., Campbell 1949; Hyde 2003) posit that universal themes are embodied in **myths**, or **legends** (see Chapter 2). Myth, in turn, is the root of storytelling, bringing the idea of universality full circle, back to plot.

In addition to being revealed in the elements of drama, a play's universality is also dependent on its **audience**. A story that attracts certain viewers might be rejected by others. For example, an audience that appreciates the classical structure of Shakespearean drama might not appreciate modern, absurdist drama with its deliberate lack of structure. A story about a historic legend in one nation will likely not play universally in other countries in which that legend is unknown.

It can be argued that universality is the primary concept of drama. If a play does not relate to its spectators, it cannot be successful. Universality, then, may be considered the overarching theoretic element that all the other elements unite to achieve.

Catharsis

Catharsis describes the audience's feelings toward a play. Does the drama draw the viewers into the story emotionally and leave them feeling satisfied in the end? Does it bring them to tears or laughter or both? Though catharsis takes place in the spectators, rather than in the drama itself, it is included here as a principle of drama because the elements of a play are what bring about catharsis in the viewers. Just as universality is the overarching objective of drama, catharsis serves as a measure of the effectiveness of a play's elements in achieving that objective.

The spectator of a drama is emotionally or intellectually "purged" as a result of experiencing the play. Aristotle discusses this concept as it applies to tragedy, noting that a tragic drama incites pity and fear. Other dramatic theorists (e.g., Nicoll 1936) further observe that, where tragedy elicits **pathos**, comedy elicits **laughter**. Laughter brings emotional relief as well as does compassion; therefore, Aristotle's original concept of catharsis may be expanded to include laughter as well as tears. Gassner (1966) expands the idea of catharsis to include **enlightenment**: The audience learns something from its experience with the drama. Abdullah (1985) reinforces the intellectual aspect of catharsis in his discussion of two general stages of the cathartic experience: "emotional excitation" and "intellectual understanding." He clarifies that "the cathartic response begins with *emotive arousal* and ends with *cognition*" (emphasis added) (9); that is, the spectators first *feel* an emotional cleansing and then they are able to *think* about the play's meaning.

The concept of catharsis is important in dramatic theory because of the ability of drama to appeal to the emotions and intellect of viewers. Through the manipulation of sentiment and ideas, the audience may experience a purgation, or catharsis, of feeling and thought. This cathartic release leaves the spectators feeling satisfied in the end. Without some release of emotion or thought, the spectators feel unsatisfied because the drama fails to engage them emotionally and intellectually. For example, in our script *La Llorona*, the audience feels emotionally cleansed at the end when the child declares his or her belief that Guadalupe has found her babies at last so that her soul can rest. Intellectually, the viewers give release to their own thoughts about guilt and eternal punishment as they reflect cognitively on the theme.

In another example, consider the television series *M★A★S★H* (1972–1983). This program succeeded in reaching the largest viewing audience of its time. A two-hour special ended the series, drawing the largest TV audience to that point in TV history: over 120 million viewers. Why did so many viewers watch each week, and especially watch the final episode? At least part of the answer is catharsis. Each week, the storylines gripped the viewers' emotions, at times frightening them, at times disgusting them, at times eliciting laughter, at times bringing tears. The viewers felt an emotional release by following the characters and their stories. At times, they also felt an intellectual release, thinking about the theme—*war destroys lives*—even after they switched off their TV sets. For the final two-hour episode, having spent a half-hour with these characters each Monday evening for a decade, the spectators wanted that final catharsis as the characters' last storylines brought closure to their time in Korea, and closure to the viewing audience's emotions and thoughts.

Style

Dramatic style has been analyzed by many scholars (e.g., Hodge 1999; McKee 2010). For this primer, it is useful to pull together the major elements of style and place them on a four-cell diagram of two dimensions: realism versus nonrealism, and tragedy versus comedy (see Figure 8.3). These dimensions may be subdivided for deeper analysis. I begin with realism and nonrealism.

Realism and Nonrealism

Some scholars (e.g., Hatlen 1991) divide **realism** into traditional realism, romanticism, and naturalism. **Naturalism** is the actual recreation of elements, such as Civil War actors who sew their uniforms using the same materials and stitching methods as Civil War soldiers. **Romanticism** employs the most-associated elements of a given setting to provide a level of realism that we think once existed, such as candle light in the window of a Victorian-style home covered by a fresh blanket of white snow. **Realism**, in addition to being the overarching term for its side of the style spectrum, more narrowly also refers

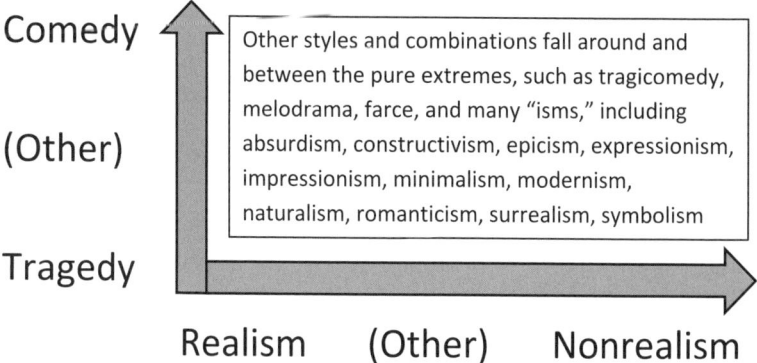

Figure 8.3 A model of dramatic styles on two axes: realism to nonrealism, and tragedy to comedy

to traditionally realistic scenic elements that represent what they are meant to be without actually being constructed naturalistically, such as muslin flats that look like realistic walls, even though they are not naturalistic walls.

On the **nonrealism** end of the spectrum, some theorists (e.g., Brecht 1927; Balazs 1953) include several stylistic categories, such as absurdism, avant-gardism, constructivism, cubism, dadaism, epicism, existentialism, expressionism, impressionism, minimalism, modernism, neorealism, post-modernism, surrealism, symbolism, and no doubt other "isms." Each is characterized by one or more particular qualities. For example, expressionism is characterized by fanciful sets and extreme contrasts of light, shadow, and contrast. Impressionism stems from a nineteenth-century school of art that favored small brushstrokes to give impressions of light and color rather than photographic realism. Surrealism is associated with dreams, utilizing vivid images and colors put together in ways that do not exist in the awake world, such as an egg melting like a vinyl record on a table in the open desert.

La Llorona lends itself to interpretation on both ends of the spectrum. On the realism end, the child's bedroom might be constructed to represent a life-like room that could be the hangout of any child, suggesting that the story is relevant to anyone. Then again, a director might choose abstraction for the bedroom, such as geometric shapes that suggest a bedroom rather than actually looking like a bedroom, to foreshadow Guadalupe's story that ends in the abstraction of a wandering soul.

Likewise, Guadalupe's village could be interpreted realistically, suggesting that her world is similar to ours. Or it could be interpreted nonrealistically, suggesting that her story takes place on a different, more abstract level of meaning than on the level of actual life. Similarly, as Guadalupe's soul wanders the earth in her nightmarish state of eternity, the costume, makeup, lighting, camera angles, and editing techniques could push the surrealism of those images.

Tragedy and Comedy

On the tragedy–comedy dimension of dramatic style, tragedy is most notably characterized by the concept of *ruin*. In tragic theory, the story takes the protagonist on a journey that ultimately leads to his or her destruction. This may conform to the classical convention that the protagonist him or herself suffers death or ruin (e.g., *Oedipus*, Sophocles 429 BCE; *Othello*, Shakespeare 1604), or the modern notion that the protagonist may suffer the death or destruction of loved ones (e.g., *Schindler's List*, Spielberg 1994; many "movies of the week" that dramatize tragic news events for television). In the case of our sample script, *La Llorona*, it is the protagonist's own actions that lead to her ruin: her choice to murder her children leads to her soul's eternal perdition.

The comedy side of the tragedy–comedy style spectrum contrasts with tragedy in that the protagonist's journey does not lead to ruin but to *success*. Everything turns out OK in the end. Only the bad guys get hurt or destroyed. The good guys triumph. We witness a happy ending.

According to comic theory (see Chapter 9), we can only laugh if there is **no real harm**. To be sure, there is harm in comedy, but it is inconsequential within the context of the story. Bad guys might get hurt or killed, but they are not the leading characters, so we are not emotionally invested in them. Note that in real life, the death or destruction of anyone leaves great sorrow in its wake for someone because someone—parent, sibling, friend—cares about that person. In the context of storytelling, however, the audience is led to care about only one or a few characters, so the audience can only feel sorrow for those principal characters. In comedy, those principals cannot suffer great or lasting harm because that would arouse sorrow rather than amusement in the viewers. Other characters, however, can experience harm and even death because the viewers have not been led to invest emotionally in them. Sometimes a leading character in a comedy does get hurt, but the hurt is not too serious and it does not last. We see the hurt get healed within the story. Or if the story ends with the character still hurt, we know that he or she will be all right after the story closes.

Some examples. *La Llorona* is not a comedy; the protagonist's soul is hurt badly. Yet, as is the case with all tragedies, there is room for some **comic relief** in appropriate moments within the otherwise sad story. The banter between parent and child in the bookend story could be embellished with some humor. The villagers who gather at Guadalupe's hut in the principal story could include some comic characters. The old hag could be interpreted as a satirical or even farcical character, pointing up the absurdity of society's rules: good satire and farce always lampoon the absurd.

Another example is *Home Alone* (Columbus 1990). The protagonist, a child named Kevin (Macaulay Culkin), is accidentally left behind when his family leaves for a Christmas holiday. The antagonists are two burglars. We laugh at this comedy because, even though it appears at times that the burglars are going to get Kevin—subclimaxes in the plot—obstacles that Kevin must overcome—we know that he will triumph in the end. No serious harm comes to Kevin. The burglars, though, undergo one painful sight gag after another. Because they're the bad guys, we can watch them get hurt and still laugh. We take pleasure in their pain, a concept called **Schadenfreude** (see Chapter 9), because they are bumbling comic characters and we know the harm is not permanent. In real life, falling on ice and getting hit by bricks and catching fire are painful experiences. In comedy, they are funny experiences, as long as they do not happen to someone about whom we care emotionally. Comic theory incorporates much more than this brief discussion about stylistic elements. Chapter 9 offers a deeper explication of comic theory, including **high and low comedy**, the three grand theories of comedy (**incongruity, superiority**, and **psychoanalytic**), and **comic structure**.

Between comedy on one end of the style spectrum and tragedy on the other, discussed above, lie other dramatic styles. A significant third style of drama is **melodrama**. This style treats its themes seriously—as in tragedy—but with humor interspersed, and the protagonist triumphs in the end—as in comedy. He or she faces serious obstacles (tragedy) but emerges without ruin (comedy). Many plays, films, and TV shows fall into this broad category. For example, *Forrest Gump* (Zemeckis 1994) is not ruined at the end of his movie; conversely, he triumphs over great adversity to arrive at his goal in the end—a normal life with a child, just as his life was normal when he was a child with his mother. Yet, this film is not a comedy. Certainly it has funny moments, but the loss the protagonist faces is not superficial and easily healed. He has lost the love of his life, whom he finally won after emerging victorious from many trials. This loss is too deep for the film to be pure comedy. Instead, the film is melodrama—serious in tone, with comic moments, and with the protagonist ending his journey successfully.

Many action movies and murder mysteries and psychological thrillers are melodramatic in that the good guys—in spite of their flaws—win in the end, but at the expense of some loss that is too great to leave us laughing. Other examples include just about any hour-long episodic television series broadly labeled as "drama" (short for "melodrama" rather than the original meaning of "conflict"), from *Bonanza*

(1959–1973) to *Dallas* (1978–1991, 2012–present) to the island of *Lost* (2004–2010) to *Homeland* (2011–present).

Another style discussed in the literature is **tragicomedy**, which offers laughs like comedy, but in which the protagonist's dilemma is not resolved, neither tragically nor comically. For example, in *Waiting for Godot* (Beckett 1954), the two buddies elicit laughter with their bumbling ways, but the end finds them exactly where they were at the beginning, no better, no worse, having learned nothing, having not seen Godot, but still waiting for him.

Summary

Together with Aristotle's six foundational elements of dramatic theory—**plot, character, theme, dialogue, sound (music)**, and **spectacle**—these five additional concepts—**unity, metaphor, universality, catharsis**, and **style**—comprise a solid foundation of dramatic theory and practice. **Unity of action and theme** is important in that all **subplots** of a story reinforce the **main plot** thematically. Unifying **metaphors** enhance the unity of drama. **Universality** is achieved when a play is relevant to its **audience members**, grabbing their interest by relating to something in their lives. **Catharsis** is the emotional and intellectual purging of feeling or satisfaction that audience members experience when a story touches them. Each play has a particular **style** somewhere at or between **realism** and **nonrealism** and at or between the pure dramatic forms of **tragedy** and **comedy**. It is important for dramatists to understand the function and creation of these eleven elements of drama. Moving from understanding to applying these concepts can guide dramatists to successful productions.

Reflection and Discussion

1. In the previous chapters' "Reflection and Discussion" exercises, you worked on a scene that expresses an important

theme in your life, including a plot, characters, dialogue, sound, and spectacle. Now use the five major concepts in this chapter to "grade" your scene. Assess how well your scene exhibits unified action that points to a unified theme. Does your scene suggest a unifying metaphor? Does the scene engage you and others who read it, demonstrating universality? Do you feel satisfied at the end of the scene—do you experience catharsis? How would you describe your scene in terms of realism and nonrealism and also tragedy and comedy—where would you place it in Figure 8.3?
2. For another "reflection and discussion" exercise in Chapter 7, you attended a stage play. Consider that play, or a different play that you have seen. Did it grab you? Why or why not? How did the director, cast, and crew attain universality, if they did, or how did they fail if the play did not relate to you? What would you say was the unifying metaphor? Was the play tragedy, comedy, or something between? Was it realistic or nonrealistic or something between?
3. What is the most engaging film or episode of a favorite television series that you have seen? What pops to mind first—one that really sticks with you? Using the concepts in this chapter, consider why that movie or TV episode was so engaging that you remember it so vividly.

9

Comedy

    This book takes its outline largely from Aristotle's *Poetics* (*c.* 335 BCE). It is believed that Aristotle divided his work into two books, one on tragedy, which survives and comprises the bulk of *Poetics*, and one on comedy, which has been lost to history, though some believe a tenth-century manuscript known as the *Tractatus Coislinianus* offers a commentary that summarizes the main points of the "second book" (Watson 2012). In the *Poetics*, Aristotle discusses all poetic drama, using Sophocles's *Oedipus Rex* (*c.* 429 BCE) as a case study to make his argument that tragedy is comprised of the six elements of all drama: plot, character, theme, dialogue, music (sound), and spectacle. Because the chapters in this book use Aristotle's foundational work about tragedy, no additional chapter on that dramatic style is necessary. However, an additional chapter about comedy is useful for writers and is presented here.

High and Low Comedy

    Contemporary comic theory has its roots in the late nineteenth and early twentieth centuries (Fink 2013, 45). Scholars studied various comic traditions, from the ancient Greeks (e.g., Aristophanes *c.* 446–386 BCE) and Romans (Plautus *c.* 254–184 BCE) (see Figure 9.1) through the Renaissance (e.g., *commedia dell'arte*, Katritsky 2006), through contemporary comedies of their day (e.g., Oscar Wilde 1854–1900; George Bernard Shaw 1856–1950; Anton Chekhov 1860–1904; Noel Coward 1899–1973). They began to analyze humor in terms of **high comedy** and **low comedy** (Charney 2005).

High comedy is also called the **comedy of manners**, referring originally to late-seventeenth-century British plays known as "Restoration Comedies" (Nettleton, Case, and Stone 1975, 149). High comedy refers to comedy of the high class. This comic style utilizes intellectual humor that relies heavily on clever dialogue, such as *The Importance of Being Earnest* (Wilde 1895) (see Figure 9.5). The idea is that the cultured and educated speak witty dialogue, so the humor arises from our watching the upper crust get their comeuppance. We get to see those with higher social status fall down harmlessly to our level through clever words (and sometimes clever **sight gags**, as well). For example, one of my favorite bits of high comedy is in Edmund

Figure 9.1 Two archetypes of ancient comedy, the Roman Plautus (c. 254-184 BCE) and the Greek Aristophanes (c. 446-386 BCE)

Rostand's *Cyrano de Bergerac* (1897), Act I Scene 4, when Cyrano insults another man for being too dimwitted to poke proper fun at Cyrano's big nose (see Figure 9.2). In insulting the dimwit, Cyrano shows how clever he is by insulting his own nose in superior fashion.

> Ah no! That's too brief, young man! You might have said . . . Oh! . . . a hundred things, to plan by varying the tone . . . for example just suppose . . . Aggressive: "I, Sir, if I had such a nose, I'd have it amputated on the spot!" Friendly: "But it must drown itself a lot, you need a drinking-bowl of a special shape!" Descriptive: "It's a rock! A peak! A cape! What's that, it's a cape? It's a peninsular!" Curious: "That oblong bag, what's it serve you for? A sheath for scissors? Or a writing case?" Gracious: "Do you love the winged race so much, that you benignly set yourself to provide their little claws with a shelf!" Insolent: "Sir, when that pipe of yours glows, does the tobacco smoke rise from your nose and make the neighbours cry, your chimney's on fire?" Considerate: "Have a care, lest your head grow tired of such a weight . . . and it's the ground you sit on!" Tender: "Have a small umbrella fashioned, for fear lest in sunshine it lose all its colour!" Pedantic: "That rare beast, Aristophanes, Sir, named Hippocamp-elephanto-camelos, must have on its head such flesh, such a solid boss!" Familiar: "The latest fashion, my friend, that crook for hanging your hat on? True, it's a useful hook!" Eloquent: "No winds at all, majestic nose can give you colds! Except when the mistral blows!" Dramatic: "When it bleeds it's the Red Sea!" Admiring: "What a sign for a perfumery!" Lyric: "Is this a conch? . . . are you a Triton?" Simple: "This monument, when does it open?" Respectful: "Sir, allow me to congratulate you. That's what we call owning a gabled view!" Rustic: "Nah! That thing a nose? No way, not it! That's a dwarf pumpkin, or a giant turnip!" Military: "Point that thing towards the cavalry!" Practical: "Do you want it entered

in the lottery? Certainly, sir, it would be the biggest prize!" Or lastly . . . parodying Pyramus's sighs: "Behold the nose that mars its owner's nature destroying harmony! It blushes now, the traitor!"—That's an idea, sir, of what you might have said, if you'd an ounce of wit or letters in your head: but of wit, O most lamentable creature, you've never had an atom, and you feature three letters only, and those three spell: Ass!

In contrast to high comedy, low comedy refers to comedy of the lower class. This category is sometimes called **slapstick** after a stage prop consisting of two flat sticks hinged at the bottom to appear as one. When an actor swings the stick, the two halves first separate on the down swing and then slap together when the swinging stops,

Figure 9.2 Edmond Rostand (1868–1918) and a drawing of Cyrano de Bergerac (1619–1655), the writer on whom he based his most famous play of the same name (1897)

making a loud crack that creates the aural illusion that the victim has really been whacked hard. Slapstick humor relies heavily on **sight gags**—visual humor that relies on actions the viewers *see* to generate laughs, as opposed to **aural gags**, which is a fancy way of saying **jokes** that the audience must hear to laugh. Examples of sight gags abound in the comedy acts of vaudeville, *Punch and Judy* puppet shows (see Figure 9.3), and *The Three Stooges* movies. Here, instead of arising from witty dialogue (though there certainly might be some clever dialogue writing), the humor comes from the visual acts of characters at odds with the situations in which they find themselves. Typically, in contrast to the high-class aristocrats of high comedy, the characters of low comedy are perceived to be below us in social status. We laugh at their unrefined, vulgar, yet harmless acts of silliness. Moe despairs of Curly's stupidity, so he hits him on the head with a hammer, only to have the hammer bounce off Curly's head and hit Moe in the eye. Lucy (*I Love Lucy* 1951–1957) gets a job at a chocolate factory where the boss is intent on maximizing output, so the conveyor belt speeds up and Lucy has to jam chocolate pieces in her mouth to keep from getting behind. Lloyd (Jim Carrey, *Dumb & Dumber* 1994) lights a fart on fire.

Figure 9.3 Punch and Judy puppet theater

Much comedy mixes elements of both high and low humor. The famous "Who's on First" comedy sketch of Bud Abbott (1895–1974) and Lou Costello (1906–1959) is an example. The skits of this comic duo incorporated lots of sight gags, springing from the low comedy tradition. But the cleverness and rapid-fire delivery of "Who's on First" borrows from the tradition of witty high comedy. The bit is made even funnier by the unexpected: two low-comedy rubes deliver this high-comedy banter.

Another example of mixing high and low comedy comes from one of my favorite TV sitcoms, *Frasier* (1993–2004). Frasier and his brother Miles were educated, upper-crust psychiatrists who spoke French and enjoyed fine wine. Their father was a beer-drinking, blue-collar cop, retired after taking a bullet in the leg. We could enjoy the brothers' high-class, witty banter, and when we didn't understand it, their father would be the voice of the audience, offering some low-class insult to put them down.

One episode finds the boys in their childhood home where they dig up a floorboard, only to find a skull. A **high comedy** send-up of the grave diggers' scene in *Hamlet* (1603) ensues. Another episode finds Frasier trying on a clown suit to treat a patient who is scared of clowns. The suit frightens his father, who suffers a minor coronary, leading them to the hospital, where Frasier's patient—who happens to be a nurse—arrives on the elevator just as Frasier—still in his clown suit—goes to that same elevator. The nurse screams, the door closes, Frasier retreats. He tries again. She's still on the elevator. Scream. Door closes. Frasier retreats. Repeat once more for a total of three *low comedy* sight gags as Frasier in the clown suit scares his patient the nurse. It is no accident that this gag happens three times—one of the principles of comic structure is the *Rule of Threes* (more later).

Schadenfreude and *Mudita*

Whether high or low or a mix of both, integral to comic theory is the notion of **schadenfreude**, (SHAH-dun-froy-duh), literally "harm joy" or "damage pleasure." This German term refers to the joy that viewers take at the misfortunes of others, sometimes called "malicious glee" (Portmann 2000, 28). However, equally important is the notion that the characters can suffer **no lasting harm** (MacHovec 2012). If a protagonist or other principal or supporting character in whom the audience is invested emotionally suffers permanent damage (e.g., Oedipus Rex blinding himself, *c*. 429 BCE) or even death (e.g., Maximus dying in *Gladiator* 2000), the viewers feel pathos rather than humor, perhaps even crying rather than laughing. However, if any harm done to a character is only temporary, such as the loss of a fortune that is regained by the end of the story, or the loss of a true love who returns in the end, or the break of an arm or leg that will heal in time, then we can laugh. Consider the age-old story of two lovers who cannot be together because they come from different backgrounds. If the lovers end up dead, as in *Romeo and Juliet* (Shakespeare 1597), *West Side Story* (stage play 1957; film 1961), and others, we cannot laugh at their misfortune. But if the lovers end up together, as in *Pretty Woman* (Marshall 1990), *Notting Hill* (Michell 1999) and others, then we can laugh at the characters' hurt because the hurt is gone by the story's end. A **happy ending** is necessary for comedy—necessary for the viewers to experience *schadenfreude* rather than tears of sorrow.

Of course, we can also take pleasure in people's good fortune as well as their bad fortune. Contrasting with **schadenfreude** is the concept of **mudita** (Fink 2013, 46). This term comes from the Buddhist tradition and is sometimes translated as "sympathetic joy" (as opposed to the "malicious joy" *of* **schadenfreude**) (Buddhist Studies 2008). We appreciate when a character we like experiences something good or positive, such as when the lovers finally get together at the end of a romantic comedy. It should be noted in this chapter on comedy that **mudita** can be experienced in all forms of drama, including tragedy. In *Gladiator* (2000), for example, we rejoice with Maximus when he is victorious in the Roman arena, even if we tear up at the end when he dies.

Three Grand Theories of Comedy: Incongruity, Superiority, and Psychoanalytic (Relief)

Comic theory today is generally discussed in terms of three broad theories: **incongruity**, **superiority**, and **psychoanalysis** or **relief** (Berger 1999; Meyer 2000; Raskin 1984; Sharrer et al. 2006, 619).

Incongruity Theory

Incongruity theory posits that laughter is elicited when two or more things are juxtaposed in new or unusual ways. This juxtaposition can take a number of forms. A **fish out of water** phenomenon occurs when a person faces obstacles outside of his or her normal world. For example, in *Elf* (Favreau 2003), Buddy (Will Ferrell), having been raised at the North Pole, travels to New York City to find his biological father. Comedy ensues as this man-sized elf learns the ways of the Big Apple. It should be noted that other forms of drama besides comedy also use the "fish out of water" technique. For example, in the drama *Midnight Express* (Parker 1978), American Billy Hayes (Brad Davis) lands in a Turkish prison for smuggling hashish and must first survive and then escape this hell. In the science fiction film *Aliens* (Cameron 1986), Ellen Ripley (Sigourney Weaver) returns to a distant planet to defeat some nasty creatures. That noted, this chapter focuses on comedy, and the *fish out of water* protagonist can be crafted by the writer to generate laughs as the hero struggles with his or her unfamiliar circumstances. Charlie Chaplin (1889–1977) mastered the *fish out of water* character with his Tramp persona who found himself in unfamiliar situations in film after film (see Figure 9.4).

An **unexpected surprise** can also elicit laughter. To be sure, in horror films the unexpected elicits a shock that can make viewers gasp or scream or jump in their seats. For example, a knife-wielding woman—or so we think—suddenly appears outside the curtain as Marion Crane

Figure 9.4 Charlie Chaplin as his famous character, "The Tramp"

(Janet Leigh) takes a shower in *Psycho* (Hitchcock 1960). In comedy horror films, the scare can give way immediately to laughs if the unexpected moment is also incongruous. In fact, according to **Excitation Transfer Theory** (Zillmann 1971), the heightened excitement of the scare can transfer to the funny surprise that follows and heighten the laughter. That is, the viewers laugh harder at the funny bit than they normally would because the preceding scare has enhanced their level of excitement. For example, *Scary Movie* (Wayans 2000) opens with a teenage girl getting a creepy phone call while home alone on Halloween (naturally). The doorbell rings, and she takes a baseball bat to confront the psycho, only to open the door (scary moment) and swing at . . . not a killer but trick-or-treaters (funny moment).

Self-reflexivity can also lead to laughs. This occurs when a visual gag or some dialogue breaks the **suspension of disbelief** by revealing or commenting on the story itself. For example, in *Annie Hall* (Allen 1977), Alvy Singer (Woody Allen) often breaks the *fourth wall*—the imaginary invisible wall through which the camera shoots—to comment to the audience about the scene.

Illogical situations also create comedy with their incongruity. We laugh when we know that something just doesn't make sense. **Satire** and **farce**, in particular, lend themselves to illogical humor. For example, consider *Monty Python's Flying Circus* (1969–1974), for my money one of the funniest sketch shows ever. In one skit, Germany versus Greece in a soccer match, with the illogical humor being that it is German philosophers of the last few centuries (e.g., Hegel, Kant, Nietsche—with Marx later subbing in) going against Greek philosophers of old (e.g., Socrates, Plato, Aristotle). They take the field, and just as the head referee, Confucius, blows the whistle to start the game, the philosophers do not kick the ball, but instead wander about the field contemplating the existence of the ball. Everyone knows the logical thing to do in soccer is to kick the ball, so this illogical behavior of the world's most logical thinkers provides wonderful comedy of the incongruous by going to the **logical extreme**—the point where the progression of events logically leads to an illogical outcome. In that outcome, the Greeks finally win when Archimedes—a mathematician—has a "eureka" idea and kicks the ball to his teammates who score a goal.

The **absurd** makes us laugh. This seems to be the first type of comedy we understand as babies, and therefore perhaps the most fundamental of all comic types. What do grownups do when they want to make a baby smile and giggle? They make silly faces. Babies are deeply tuned into faces (especially their parents') as they first begin to understand their world, so the absurdity of contorting those faces elicits laughter: the more absurd, the heartier the laugh. An example comes once again from the *Monty Python* troupe. Michael Palin enters an argument clinic and is directed to John Cleese who merely contradicts everything Palin says. Palin argues that contradiction is not argument, to which Cleese responds that it is. The absurdity escalates until time runs out. Palin argues that his time is not up, but Cleese is off the clock and cannot argue anymore. Palin pays Cleese for five more minutes, at which point Cleese argues that Palin did not pay, but Palin argues he did pay, otherwise Cleese would not be arguing. After more silly contradictions, Palin leaves to register a complaint and ends up in a wrong room where bureaucratic inspectors arrive and hit everyone on the head. Blissful nonsense.

Exaggeration plays a key role in incongruous absurdity. Permit me one more example from the *Monty Python* television series. In one of the group's best-known skits that lampoons government bureaucracy to the exaggerated extreme, John Cleese walks about London in the silliest of ways, arriving at his office in the Ministry of Silly Walks, where Michael Palin is waiting to apply for a government grant to develop his own silly walk. Palin demonstrates his walk, and Cleese observes that it is not particularly silly. Palin insists that he can make it sillier with funding. Cleese shows him a film reel of silly walks and then offers him a "research fellowship on the Anglo-French silly walk." The sketch ends with an exaggerated satire of French silliness. Perhaps this skit is remembered so fondly because it incorporates so many elements of comedy: the absurdity of a man walking in this most ridiculous fashion; the unexpected surprise of this man on the staid streets of London; the exaggeration of both the walk and the notion of the government having a ministry for something as illogical—or logically extreme—as silly walks; the low comedy of the sight gag of the various walks; and the high comedy of the witty banter about whether or not Palin's walk is silly enough. All these comic elements together make the point (theme) of the pointlessness of bureaucracy.

Stereotypes can be considered as yet another aspect of incongruity theory. Much comedy relies on readily recognized, and often exaggerated, stereotypes of people or groups of people. Stereotyping is rarely accurate, of course, because it relies on applying broad brush stroke characteristics that cannot take into account the unique qualities of each person. At its worst, stereotyping can be harmful to individuals or groups. At its best, however, stereotyped characters provide the viewers with an instant "type" that does not need to be developed and, therefore, can get an immediate laugh. Using *Monty Python's* "Ministry of Silly Walks" sketch once more, the stereotype of a bureaucrat who wears a suit and carries a briefcase to his office sets up the comedy well as this man with a government desk job walks in the most nonsensical of ways.

Superiority Theory

A second grand theory of comedy is **superiority theory**. This posits that viewers laugh when they feel better than others (Berger 1999; Feinberg 1978; Grotjahn 1966; Gruner 1999; Keough 1998; Meyer 2000; Morreall 2009; Rapp 1951; Ziv 1984). We audience members are triumphant in our pursuits; whereas, the rubes of comedy fail time and time again—until the final, triumphant resolution, of course. It is useful here to consider that dramatists, whether serious or comic, have only two means to convey their stories to their audiences: **action** and **dialogue**. That is, everything must be revealed in what characters on the stage or screen *do* and in what they *say*. To be sure, the setting and sounds add visual spectacle and audio atmosphere to the story, but a story with only a set and music and sound effects is not a story until characters appear and do something and/or speak words. Screenwriters must create actions and words that tell their stories, whatever the format: comedy, tragedy, tragicomedy, melodrama, or something else.

Applying the dramatic vehicles of dialogue and action to the superiority theory of comedy, it is in the words and behaviors of the characters that the writer makes the audience feel better than those characters. In **high comedy**, for example, the witty and often silly banter of the educated characters reveals them to be no better than, and perhaps ultimately stupider than, their less-educated viewers. In Oscar Wilde's *The Importance of Being Earnest* (1895), Algernon Moncrieff sends his servant to get a cigarette case that John Worthing (nickname Ernest) left at Algernon's home earlier (see Figure 9.5). This dialogue exchange occurs:

Figure 9.5 Oscar Wilde (1854–1900), and a photograph from the original London production of his play, *The Importance of Being Earnest* (1895)

JOHN: Do you mean to say you have had my cigarette case all this time? I wish to goodness you had let me know. I have been writing frantic letters to Scotland Yard about it. I was very nearly offering a large reward.

ALGERNON: Well, I wish you would offer one. I happen to be more than usually hard up.

JOHN: There is no good offering a large reward now that the thing is found.

[Servant enters with the cigarette case. then exits.]

ALGERNON: I think that is rather mean of you, Ernest, I must say. [Opens case and examines it.] However, it makes no matter, for, now that I look at the inscription inside, I find that the thing isn't yours after all.

JOHN: Of course it's mine. You have seen me with it a hundred times, and you have no right whatsoever to read what is written inside. It is a very ungentlemanly thing to read a private cigarette case.

ALGERNON: Oh! It is absurd to have a hard and fast rule about what one should read and what one shouldn't. More than half of modern culture depends on what one shouldn't read.

JOHN: I am quite aware of the fact, and I don't propose to discuss modern culture. It isn't the sort of thing one should talk of in private. I simply want my cigarette case back.

We laugh at the absurd foppishness of these two going on about proper cigarette case etiquette, knowing that we would never stoop to such banality (now would we, smile smile?).

In **low comedy**, the viewers feel superior to the rubes whose actions are beneath them. For example, in the ancient Greek play *Lysistrata* (Aristophanes 411 BCE), men walk about with giant prosthetic erections underneath their cloaks because their wives have denied them sex until they end the Peloponnesian War. In vaudevillian comedy, the players engage in all kinds of hitting and falling down. In *The Simpsons* television series (1989–present), father Homer chokes son Bart in one **running gag**—a visual or dialogue joke that re-occurs from time to time for laughs. We howl at such zany antics because, after all, we would never be as stupid as those characters (now would we, smile smile?). We feel superior, so we laugh.

Psychoanalytic or Relief Theory

A third grand comic theory is **psychoanalytic theory**, sometimes called **relief theory**. Here, scholars argue that we laugh to release nervous energy brought on by what we see and hear, thereby reducing our stress (Berlyne 1972, 50–53; Morreall 2009; Schaeffer 1981). This is a **catharsis** of feeling applied to comedy. Shurcliff notes that "the greater the subjects' anxiety prior to relief, the greater . . . the judged humor" (1968, 362). Scharrer et al. write that "people laugh at things that make them uncomfortable (e.g., aging, violence) or guilty (e.g., sex)" (2006, 619). Freud (1905; 1922) posited that laughter is a means of releasing forbidden feelings, allowing for pleasure. We find humor in watching someone else take a beating because that releases our own hidden hostilities, or in watching people have sex because that releases our own sexual desires.

Central to psychoanalytic theory is the notion that the characters can suffer **no lasting harm**, as previously discussed. We can laugh to release anxiety, stress, nervous energy, and hidden feelings because no major characters remain hurt in the end. To be sure, some characters do suffer greatly, and even die, in comedy, but they are either minor characters in whom we are not emotionally invested, or they are the bad guys whose demise we enjoy watching because they deserve it. For example, in the Coen brothers' dark comedy *Fargo* (1996), two hired kidnappers kill a trooper who stops their car. The trooper is only in this scene, so the audience does not get to know him, making his death acceptable in a comedy. Later, after the audience has grown accustomed to the two killers, one kills the other and feeds his dead body into a wood chipper. The audience roars in laughter at this **dark comedy** or **gallows humor**—comedy that stems from the dark side of the human psyche, often relating to death—because the body was one of the bad guys who got what was coming to him. The heroine of the story, police chief Marge Gunderson (Frances McDormand), then shoots the other bad guy in the leg when he runs, again acceptable because he, too, is a murderer. Note that this film would not be a comedy (dark as it is) if chief Gunderson were killed and fed into the wood chipper because the audience is too emotionally invested in her "good guy" principal character.

The concept of **schadenfreude**, discussed previously, is also part and parcel of psychoanalytic theory. We take malicious joy in the sufferings of others because that helps us release our own suffering. Again though, others' suffering can only be funny if it is *not lasting*, or if permanent suffering occurs only to minor characters and antagonists (bad guys). In comedy, protagonists (heroes) must return to normal at the end for us to enjoy our **schadenfreude** at their expense. For example, in the *Pink Panther* films and television series, bumbling French inspector Jacques Clouseau (played by various actors including Peter Sellers and Steve Martin) takes a lot of physical abuse, whether at the hands of his servant, his supervisor, the bad guy, or even a love interest. We delight in his pain, but only because he always gets up for his next mishap, and we know he'll "get his man" (or woman) in the end.

Comic Structure

Having examined the three grand theories of comedy—incongruity, superiority, psychoanalytic (relief)—this chapter turns to an exploration of comic structure—setting up and paying off laughs. It is important for comedy writers to understand and apply the techniques of delivering comic moments to their audiences.

Setup and Payoff

The overarching concept of comic structure is the **setup and payoff**. In truth, this is the case with all forms of dramatic writing. The author must introduce something that makes the audience wonder what will happen next—the setup—and then eventually deliver what happens—the payoff. For example, in the drama *Citizen Kane* (Welles 1941), the dying Charles Foster Kane utters the word, "Rosebud," setting in motion the reporter's—and audience's—desire to learn the significance of that word. The payoff comes at the end when Rosebud is revealed.

All types of comedy bits benefit from this overarching setup–payoff structure, whether physical sight gags, witty dialogue, outright jokes, or whatever. In the beginning of *Raiders of the Lost Ark* (Spielberg 1981), Indiana Jones (Harrison Ford) uses his whip to disarm a man with a pistol. Later, Jones encounters a sword-wielding terrorist, and the audience—having been set up—anticipates a fight scene in which Jones will somehow disarm the swordsman with his whip. Instead, the payoff is even better and funnier because it is unexpected. Jones reaches into his holster, takes out a pistol, and shoots the terrorist.

Rule of Threes

Within the overarching **setup–payoff** structure, some additional considerations are important for writing comedy. One is the **Rule of Threes**. The idea stems from joke telling, in which some types of story jokes (not riddles or one-liners or other types) consist of three beats, or moments. The first two are the **setup**, establishing a pattern that leads the listeners to anticipate something. The third beat delivers a twist on the anticipation, from which the laughter arises. In a typical joke, that's the **punch line**, which delivers the **payoff**. It must be noted that this "rule" is just a guideline and it applies only to some jokes. Rather than a film example to illustrate the Rule of Threes (there are many), allow me to tell you a joke that uses this principle. I hope my readers are not too offended by a little religious humor that incorporates mild *innuendo* (more on innuendo later). You can fill in other religious denominations to your liking if you choose to retell this joke.

> Three pastors—a Baptist, a Methodist, and a Lutheran—die with their wives and go to heaven. Saint Peter asks the first couple why they should be allowed to enter. The man says, "On earth, I was a Baptist minister." Saint Peter answers, "Not good enough. All you ever cared about was money." The man replies, "That's not true." Saint Peter responds, "Really? Tell me, what's your wife's name?" The man answers, "Penny." "Off you go," says Saint Pete.
>
> The Methodist and his wife are next. "Why should I let you in?" asks St. Peter. "On earth, I was a Methodist minister," the man answers. "Not good enough," says St. Pete, "all you ever cared about was drinking." The man replies, "Not true!" "Really," asks St. Pete, "then tell me, what's your wife's name?" The man answers, "Sherry." "Off you go," says Saint Pete.
>
> With that, the Lutheran minister looks at his wife and says, "We might as well go now, Fanny."

Do you see how the first two, the Baptist and the Methodist (substitute any other denominations), are the first two beats of the story, setting up the pattern? The third, the Lutheran (substitute your favorite denomination), then provides the punch line, or payoff. If only one of the first two were included, just the Baptist or just the Methodist, there would be no pattern to set up the joke. If more than two were included, those extras would be superfluous, dragging out the joke unnecessarily. The joke only needs two points for the setup so the third point can be the punch line.

Running Gag

A special application of the Rule of Threes is the running gag. Here, a sight gag or a line of dialogue is repeated at critical moments in the story, setting up a laugh the first time and paying it off with more reoccurrences. While a running gag can benefit from the Rule of Threes by occurring three times, sometimes the gag can also be created with just two occurrences, or maybe the story calls for four or even more. An example of a visual running gag can be found in *My Big Fat Greek Wedding* (Zwick 2002). Gus Portokalos (Michael Constantine) has an obsession with Windex. He seems to carry a bottle wherever he goes, pulling it out at key moments in the story for a running gag—and metaphorically representing his desire for cleanliness, which underscores his desire to keep pure Greek blood in the family by preventing his daughter from marrying a non-Greek man. An example of a running gag in dialogue is in the catchphrases of many television characters, such as Homer Simpson's recurring, "D'oh!"

Double Whammy

Also stemming from joke telling is humor that benefits from a double punch, often called a double whammy. The idea here is that after the joke has been set up and the punch line has delivered the payoff, an unexpected second punch line or ending occurs. As with the

Rule of Threes, this is merely a guideline that works for only some humor. Here is an example of a joke with a double whammy:

> Two men, Idiot and Moron, rent a boat and go fishing. They have a great day and catch a lot. At the end of the day, they return the boat. As they leave, Idiot says to Moron, "That was a great fishing spot! Did you mark it so we can go back there tomorrow?" Moron answers, "Sure did. I put an 'X' in the bottom of the boat." Idiot replies, "You moron, what if we don't get the same boat tomorrow?"

You see the first punch line or single whammy—Moron is so stupid he marked the fishing spot by marking the boat, which, of course, is no longer in the fishing spot. The second punch line, or double whammy, is that Idiot is even stupider, not concerned that the boat is no longer in the same spot but concerned that they might not get the same boat.

Innuendo and Double Entendre

Some humor relies on sexual jokes. Two terms have evolved that refer to specific types of sexual humor. **Innuendo** refers to word play—usually a hint or sly remark—that insinuates, but does not outright state, a suggestion of something sexual. Mae West utters a famous line of innuendo in *She Done Him Wrong* (Sherman 1933): "Why don't you come up sometime and see me?"—often misquoted as, "Why don't you come up and see me sometime?" The TV series *Modern Family* (2009–present) is rife with innuendo. In one episode, Phil Dunphy (Ty Burrell) grows a beard, but his wife Claire (Julie Bowen) does not like it and sends him away to shave it off. He shaves it down to a horseshoe moustache or quasi-goatee, but she insists, "All of it." He replies, "Sure you don't want to dance with the devil before I get rid of it?" Here, of course, "dance with the devil" means "have sex."

A **double entendre** (pronounced in French DUBE-ul ahn-TAN-druh) is a word or phrase with two meanings, one of them sexual. Whereas innuendo merely infers something sexual, a double entendre is an actual statement of words that mean both something sexual and something else. A well-known example comes again from Mae West lore in *She Done Him Wrong* (1933), though this time it is a famous misquote that she never spoke in that film: "Is that a pistol in your pocket or are you just glad to see me?" Here, the pistol refers literally to a handgun, but in context it also refers to an erection. This line has been parodied many times, as in *Blazing Saddles* (Brooks 1974) when Lili Von Shtupp (Madeline Kahn) says, "Is that a ten-gallon hat, or are you just enjoying the show?" Other double entendres abound in *Blazing Saddles*, such as when an old friend meets the supposedly dead Sheriff Bart (Cleavon Little) and says to him, "They said you was hung," to which Bart replies, "And they was right." Here, "hung" means both "hanged to death" and "has a large penis." In the "Ministry of Silly Walks" sketch from *Monty Python* mentioned previously, John Cleese calls his secretary to bring two coffees. Her name is Mrs Two Lumps, referring both to the number of sugar cubes he wants and to her breasts.

One-Liners and Put-Downs

The above examples demonstrate that a joke can sometimes be just one line, though as with all comic structure, that one line must be set up for it to pay off with laughs. Perhaps the most famous **one-liner** is comedian Henny Youngman's, "Take my wife—please." One particular type of one-liner is the **put-down**, in which one person asserts superiority over the other with a witty insult. Winston Churchill (1874–1965) is attributed with two famous put-downs, both more legend than fact. In one, Lady Nancy Astor is said to have insulted Churchill by saying, "If I were married to you, I'd put poison in your tea," to which Churchill retorted, "If I were married to you, I'd drink it." In another, Lady Bessie Braddock accused Churchill, "Sir, you are drunk," and Churchill replied, "Madam, you are ugly, but in the morning I'll be sober" (there are variations of these). Turning to an example in film, and continuing with the tradition of British wit, in *Monty Python and the Holy Grail* (Gilliam and Jones 1975), John Cleese—as a taunting French guard atop a castle wall—insults King Arthur below with a string of put-downs, among them, "I fart in your general direction. Your mother was a hamster, and your father stank of elderberries."

Summary

Comic theory includes a host of concepts about why we laugh. **High comedy** pokes fun at upper-crust folks getting their comeuppance. **Low comedy** skewers low-class folks engaging in **sight gags** and **slapstick**. **Schadenfreude** refers to the malicious pleasure we get when we watch staged harm done to others, but only as long as sympathetic characters suffer **no lasting harm**. **Mudita** refers to the joy we take when things go well for others.

Three grand theories of comedy attempt to get at the underlying causes of laughter. **Incongruity theory** includes a *fish out of water*, an **unexpected surprise**, **self-reflexivity**, **illogical situations** and **logical extremes**, the **absurd**, **exaggeration**, and **stereotypes**. *Superiority theory* posits that viewers laugh when they are made to feel better than the characters they are observing, both in **action** *(visual gags)* and **dialogue** *(aural gags, a.k.a. jokes)*. **Psychoanalytic** or **relief theory** suggests that laughter is a **catharsis** that allows audiences to release their guilt and anxieties by watching others' foibles.

In terms of **comic structure**, it is important for writers to **set up and pay off** their audiences. Some ways to do this include the **Rule of Three**s, **running gags**, **double whammies**, **innuendo** and **double entendre**, **one-liners**, and **put-downs**. I conclude with a third joke (**Rule of Threes**) that incorporates three of these concepts: the **Rule of Threes**, the unexpected, and even a little superiority. I hope some clean religious humor is once again acceptable.

A man is trapped in his house during a flood. A truck drives by on the street and the rescuer says, "Climb in, I'll take you to safety." The man refuses, answering, "I trust God to save me." The water rises and the man is forced up to the second story. A boat comes by and a rescuer hollers, "Hop in, we'll take you to safety." The man replies, "No thank you, I trust God to save me." The water continues to rise. The man is stranded on his rooftop. A helicopter arrives and a ladder is dropped down. A rescuer yells, "Climb up, we'll take you to safety." The man answers, "No thank you, I trust God to save me." The waters rise even more, and the man drowns. He goes to heaven and meets God. He says, "God, I don't understand. I trusted you to save me. Why didn't you?" God answers, "I sent you a truck, a boat, and a helicopter. What more did you want?"

Reflection and Discussion

1. In the "Reflection and Discussion" exercises of the previous chapters, you developed a scene using all the elements of drama. If that scene is already a comedy, use the principles in this chapter to adjust it and revise it and make it better. If that scene is not a comedy, consider how you could rewrite it to make it a comic scene with the concepts presented here.
2. Think of your favorite joke. Using the concepts in this chapter, which of them apply? Now make up a new joke of your own. Many have said that you cannot write a joke from a formula; instead, you just write what is funny, as evidenced by comedy writers who approach their craft in many different ways (e.g., Desberg and Davis 2010). I agree to a point, but I think once you come up with something funny, you can refine and improve the joke or gag or scene by

understanding comedy and applying its theory and structure. Your creative process to come up with something funny can start anywhere: read to borrow ideas or to lampoon something; observe life around you for inspiration; reflect on what makes you laugh and use those bits as springboards for new bits; recruit a writing partner or team to banter about (as the writing staffs of sitcoms do); or do whatever works for you. Once you have your idea for a joke, apply the concepts in this chapter to make it great.

3. Consider your favorite comedy film or television show. Use the first one that comes to mind. How would you analyze the humor according to the principles of comic theory and structure presented here?

10

Script Formats

The previous chapters explore the foundational elements of dramatic theory and structure for all story formats, whether tragic or comic, melodramatic or tragic-comic, real or absurd, serious or humorous This chapter concludes the book by presenting a primer of the applied guidelines for formatting your scripts (adapted in part from Medoff and Fink 2012). Use these guidelines to lay out your scripts on the page.

It should be noted that most writers work out their stories before they write a fully formatted script. They often begin with an **outline** of the scenes and action within the scenes, moving things around (sometimes old school on 3 × 5 cards; sometimes on a computer), revising and rewriting as they develop their characters and plot. Following an outline of all the story points, the writer moves to a **treatment**—fleshing out the outline into something like a short story version of the pending screenplay—remembering to describe action and dialogue rather than inner thoughts because a screenplay is not a short story. Treatments are always written in the present tense, as if the action is unfolding on the screen right now (rather in the past or the future), with the scenes described in the order they are to appear on screen. Also, consistent with script formats (below), the first time a character appears in a treatment his or her name is CAPITALIZED. The writer can copyright the treatment and shop it around, looking for a buyer before writing the screenplay, or he or she can move to the screenplay when ready.

When you are ready to write your full screenplay, you may use this chapter as a format guide. Because this text is a primer, the fundamental scriptwriting "rules" are presented here; however, if you encounter a situation that is not covered by these basics, please consult a more detailed guide to screenplay formats: there are many, so a simple search for "screenplay format" will yield a number of resources, both in print and online. Additionally, you might consider using screenwriting software that formats your scripts. A popular freeware program is Celtx. The best-selling program, recommended by the Writers' Guild, is Final Draft, and another popular program is Movie Magic. Of course, you can use a word-processing program (e.g., Microsoft Word) and tab over for proper indentation, change to ALL CAPS where needed, and so on. If you know how to use templates, you can create a template or search to see if you can download a template for screenwriting for your software. You can also search for sample screenplays in the correct format and follow those as examples. Two recommended sites are Drew's Script-O-Rama and Simply Scripts.

Before you decide on any software program, consider who else might read your screenplay. If you have a writing partner and you need to share drafts of your work, you'll both need to have the same program to open and revise your work. If you plan to submit to an agent who does not have the same program, you'll need to submit in a program the agent can open. It is best to use a program that allows you to convert your script to the Adobe "Portable Document Format," or PDF, as the programs mentioned above do. This standard file format preserves the page formatting of the document, and it can be opened and read on any computer.

Screenplay Format

The screenplay format is used for movies of any length, as well as episodic television that uses the single-camera, or film-style, approach to production: each scene is recorded a number of times from different camera angles and edited together in postproduction. Note: single-camera television series—both drama and comedy—unlike film, often indicate the **act breaks**, as is the case with many multi-camera sitcom scripts. While the specifics vary, typically the words "<u>END ACT ONE</u>" appear double-spaced below the last line of Act 1, followed at the top of a *new page* with "<u>ACT TWO</u>," both designations in ALL CAPS, underlined, and centered, with another double space before the first slug line of Act 2. The screenplay format presented here is the **master scene** format used for **spec scripts**, or "speculative screenplays": unsolicited scripts written with no commission. These can be used as samples in a writer's portfolio to demonstrate his or her skill; they can be labors of love—the story the writer always wanted to tell; and they can also be scripts that a writer hopes to sell eventually at a **pitch meeting** where he or she attempts to persuade a buyer to purchase the scripts. **Commissioned scripts**—those written on assignment for pay when the writer is hired by a studio or network or independent company or producer—also use this master scene format.

Once a writer has finished **rewriting** a script—making the revisions he or she wants or that the buyer requests in **development**—the process of working out character problems and story kinks, then the script moves to a **production script**. Here, additional information is added to the script in preparation for shooting (e.g., each scene or *slug line*—see below—is numbered sequentially on the left and right margins). The detail of a production script, however, is not necessary when a writer first drafts a script in the master scene format.

For this screenplay format, the script of *La Llorona* serves as an example. Note that the first page is the **fly page**, or *cover page*, or *title* *page*. All scripts in all formats have a fly page that includes the title and author. Beyond that, the cover page might include the original source if the screenplay is an adaptation, a copyright notice, contact information, and other information the writer or company desires. Once the title graphic is created, future versions of the script often use that graphic for the fly page. There are a few differences in margins and spacing for the title pages of different script formats, which you can easily find by searching for the format in which you are writing. For the purposes of this text, you may use the fly page from *La Llorona* as a sample for most spec scripts.

Likewise, the second page of the full *La Llorona* script in Chapter 1 includes the theme, **log line** (one-sentence condensation), **synopsis** (slightly longer summary), and a character list. You may or may not include these items, depending on who you think might read your script. The television and stage-play formats usually include cast lists, and the sitcom format in particular includes a list of characters in each scene (more on the sitcom format later). If you wish to include this additional information, you may use the second page of *La Llorona* as a sample.

To illustrate the screenplay format itself, the remaining pages of *La Llorona* in Chapter 1 serve as an example. Because the full script is presented in that chapter, only the first two pages of the script itself are reproduced here for easy reference in Figure 10.1.

Margins: one-inch around the page, which means a 1.5-inch left margin to account for the 1/2 inch lost to *brads*, which are used to bind long-form scripts that are three-hole punched with one brad in the top hole and one in the bottom hole.

Type font: Courier New 12-point, which is a fixed-width, serif font with 10 characters per inch, similar to "pica" on typewriters back in the day, yielding about one page per one screen minute.

```
FADE IN:

INT. BEDROOM — NIGHT

A CHILD sleeps. Perhaps MUSIC plays. The SOUND OF MOURNFUL WIND
is heard. The child's eyes open wide.

                        CHILD
                 Mama! Mama! [or Papa! Papa!]

                        PARENT (O.S.)
                 Yes, my child, I'm coming.

PARENT enters.

                        PARENT
                      (continuing)
                 What is it, sweetheart?

                        CHILD
                 The wind, Mama [Papa]. The wind
                 sounds strange, like someone is
                 crying.

                        PARENT
                 Ah, la Llorona.

                        CHILD
                 What is la Llorona?

                        PARENT
                 La Llorona means "the weeping
                 woman." It's an old, old legend.

                        CHILD
                 Tell me, Mama [Papa]. Please tell
                 me so I can sleep.

The parent settles onto the child's bed.

                        PARENT
                 A long time ago, a beautiful woman
                 named Guadalupe lived in a village.

EXT. VILLAGE — DAY OR NIGHT

VILLAGERS are gathered around a hut, MUMBLING.
```

Figure 10.1 Sample first pages of the screenplay format

                        PARENT (O.S.)
                        (continuing)
                    She had no husband.

SCREAMS OF CHILDBIRTH come from within the hut. An OLD HAG steps
out excitedly. MUSIC PLAYS.

                            OLD HAG
                    Twins! Guadalupe has given birth to
                    twins. A boy and a girl. But these
                    twins are cursed. They have no
                    Papa.

The villagers mumble in agreed shame and shunning and then
disperse. The MUSIC builds to a FOREBODING CRESCENDO.

EXT. VILLAGE - DAY

The MUSIC TRANSITIONS to a new day. The hut sits alone. The door
opens. A figure emerges. It is GUADALUPE. She carries a basket,
from which comes the SOUND OF CRYING BABIES.

As she walks through the village, the old hag and the villagers
gather around her, forming a gantlet. They CURSE and HISS at her.
She walks through the crowd to the edge of the village. She keeps
walking.

EXT. RIVER - DAY

Guadalupe walks to the river, alone now. She sets down the basket
and stares at the water. The SOUND OF CRYING BABIES continues
from the basket.

ANGLES ON HER FACE, THE BASKET, THE WATER, PERHAPS THE SKY

Guadalupe begins to HUM A LULLABY. She reaches for the basket,
taking from it two BABIES, wrapped in cloths. She walks slowly
into the water, humming her melody. The BABIES' CRIES SUBSIDE.

Guadalupe takes a breath and submerges herself with her babies.
THE WATER ROILS AND STIRS TO A FRENZY. MUSIC CRESCENDOS.
Guadalupe's head emerges. She remains in the water, submerged to
her neck, straining and shaking violently.
Slowly, she stops shaking, tears streaking down her face. THE
WATER ALSO SETTLES, AS DOES THE MUSIC.

Figure 10.1 (*continued*)

Page numbers: beginning with *page 2*, number each page in the top right-hand corner, followed by a period.

Page breaks: avoid breaking pages in the middle of dialogue; however, this might be necessary in the case of a lengthy line. If this happens, write "(MORE)" in ALL CAPS and parentheses below the last line of dialogue on the first page, indented one inch (like a parenthetical—see below), and then write the character name again on the top of the next page (usual indentation—see below), followed by "(cont'd)" in lowercase and parentheses.

FADE IN: always begin with "FADE IN:" at the left margin, ALL CAPS, followed by a colon, and then double- or triple-space.

Slug line: identifies each new scene by describing the setting in abbreviated form; every change of location or time requires one. ALL CAPS. Three parts: (1) always begin with either "INT." or "EXT." (abbreviations for "interior" or "exterior," followed by a period); (2) next, a one- or two-word description of the location, such as "BEDROOM"; (3) follow this with a space, a hyphen, another space, and then either "DAY" or "NIGHT." Full example: "INT. BEDROOM - NIGHT." Some writers use "MORNING," "LATE AFTERNOON," "DUSK," and the like, but it is preferred that you use only "DAY" or "NIGHT"; then, only if necessary for the story, describe the more precise time in the action line that follows, after a double space.

Action line: sometimes called ***description line***, describes the scene and any action, such as, "A CHILD sleeps." Keep it brief. Include only information necessary for character and story. Details of sets, lights, wardrobe, props, and so on are left to the design team. Name the characters in this scene, and *if it is the first time they appear in the script*, CAPITALIZE THEIR NAMES. Also CAPITALIZE MUSIC, SOUND EFFECTS, and VISUAL EFFECTS, such as CAMERA MOVES. Single-space the action line, but follow it with a double space.

Character line: write out the name of the character who speaks, ALL CAPS, indented about 2.5 inches from left margin.

Parenthetical: a one- or two-word description of how the character says the line, such as "(angrily)," or to indicate the character continues speaking after an action line, "(continuing)." Use sparingly, only when truly essential—if your script is written well, a good actor will provide a good line reading without prompting. Lowercase, in parentheses, single-spaced below character line, about 2 inches from *both left and right margins*, or 1/2 inch left of character line.

Dialogue: the words that the character speaks. Lowercase, single-spaced below parenthetical (if used) or character line, indent about 1.5 inches from *both left and right margins.* Follow with a double space for the next action or slug line.

Transitions: the type of effect used to go from one scene to another, such as a **dissolve** or **wipe**. Write sparingly or not at all: the director decides the transitions. You need not write "CUT" because a straight cut is the most-used transition and it is assumed, unless a different transition is indicated. If you indicate a different transition, such as "DISSOLVE TO:" put it on the *right* margin, ALL CAPS, followed by a colon, double-spaced below the previous line. Double space again for the next slug line.

FADE OUT.: always end the script with "FADE OUT." in ALL CAPS, followed by a period, on the *right* margin.

Shorthand

(O.S.): off-screen; used when a person speaks, but is not seen, as on the other end of a telephone. (O.S.) appears on the character line after the name.

(V.O.): voice-over; used when a character speaks what is in his or her head, such as narration, flashbacks, and dream sequences. (V.O.) also appears on character line.

(beat): indicates a pause. Use sparingly; actors know when to pause in a well-written script. Format "(beat)" as a parenthetical (lowercase, in parentheses, single-spaced below character or dialogue line, indented about 2 inches from left margin—about 1/2 inch left of character line).

Ellipsis: three periods with spaces between them . . . use when a character does not complete his or her dialogue . . .

Three dashes: – – – (with spaces between them), use when a character's dialogue is cut off by another character – – –

Underlining: use underlining to add emphasis to words in dialogue, such as "I never saw you before." Use sparingly; again, actors know what words to emphasize in a well-written script.

ANGLE: a modified slug line used to indicate a change of camera perspective within a scene. Format as a slug line: left margin, ALL CAPS, double space above and below. If necessary, describe the specific angle (e.g., high angle, low angle) in an action line.

CLOSE ON: another modified slug line used to indicate a close-up on some person or object, such as "CLOSE ON BASKET."

INSERT: another modified slug line used to draw attention to something within a scene, such as "INSERT—CROSS."

POV: point of view; another modified slug line used to indicate a camera perspective of what a character sees, such as "POV—GUADALUPE."

MONTAGE: another modified slug line used to indicate a series of usually brief shots that convey a moment, such as "MONTAGE—GUADALUPE WANDERS," followed by an action line that describes the kinds of images in the montage.

Sitcom Format

The sitcom format is a modified version of the screenplay format. Note that this format is for those sitcoms specifically shot in front of a live audience with multiple cameras (e.g., *Big Bang*

Theory 2007–present). Comedies that shoot single-camera, film-style (e.g., *Modern Family* 2009–present) use the screenplay format for scripts, but often with act breaks indicated, as discussed previously. Additionally, some production companies might require some other format items unique to that production. If *La Llorona* were a multi-cam, live-audience sitcom, a sample script page might look like Figure 10.2.

The sitcom format differs from the screenplay format in the following ways. As can be seen in comparing Figures 10.1 and 10.2, the sitcom format has more blank space on each page. This is because live-audience sitcoms have a tight shooting schedule—one week per episode—and people need to write notations on the fly during rehearsal (e.g., dialogue changes, blocking notes). To be sure, the cast and crew of single-camera television and film shoots also need to write notes on their scripts, but the live-audience sitcom format requires even more blank space.

> <u>Sequential lettering of scenes</u>: <u>A</u>, <u>B</u>, <u>C</u>, and so on. Each letter appears above the slug line, CAPITALIZED, <u>underlined</u>, and centered, with at least a double space above and below it.
> <u>Slug line</u>: just like film script (INT. or EXT. - LOCATION - DAY or NIGHT), but also <u>underlined</u>.
> <u>Character list</u>: list the characters for each scene, in parentheses, one space below the slug line.
> <u>Action lines</u>: action and description lines are in ALL CAPS, unlike in film scripts; additionally, <u>underline</u> each character's first appearance and special visual and sound effects.
> <u>Character line</u>: indented about 2.5 inches and in ALL CAPS, just like film scripts.
> <u>Dialogue</u>: indented about 1.5 inches from each margin, like film scripts, but also double-spaced.

Two-Column, Split-Page, AV Format

The **two-column** script format, also called the **split-page** format and the **AV** format (audio-visual), is used for many in-studio

ACT ONE

SCENE A

FADE IN:

INT. BEDROOM — NIGHT
(Child, Parent)

A CHILD SLEEPS. PERHAPS MUSIC PLAYS. THE SOUND OF MOURNFUL WIND IS HEARD. THE CHILD'S EYES OPEN WIDE.

          CHILD

    Mama! Mama! [or Papa! Papa!]

          PARENT (O.S.)

    Yes, my child, I'm coming.

PARENT enters.

          PARENT (CONT'D)

    What is it, sweetheart?

          CHILD

    The wind, Mama [Papa]. The wind

    sounds strange, like someone is

    crying.

          PARENT

    Ah, la Llorona.

          CHILD

    What is la Llorona?

          PARENT

    La Llorona means "the weeping
    woman." It's an old, old legend.

Figure 10.2 Sample first pages of the sitcom format

                        CHILD

                Tell me, Mama [Papa]. Please

                tell me so I can sleep.

THE PARENT SETTLES ONTO THE CHILD'S BED.

                        PARENT

                A long time ago, a beautiful

                woman named Guadalupe lived

                in a village. She had no

                husband.

                       [NEW PAGE]

                        SCENE B

EXT. VILLAGE - DAY OR NIGHT

VILLAGERS ARE GATHERED AROUND A HUT, MUMBLING. SCREAMS OF
CHILDBIRTH COME FROM WITHIN THE HUT. AN OLD HAG STEPS OUT
EXCITEDLY. MUSIC PLAYS.

                        OLD HAG

                Twins! Guadalupe has given

                birth to twins. A boy and a

                girl. But these twins are

                cursed. They have no Papa.

THE VILLAGERS MUMBLE IN AGREED SHAME AND SHUNNING AND THEN
DISPERSE. THE MUSIC BUILDS TO A FOREBODING CRESCENDO.

Figure 10.2 (continued)

multi-camera productions, as well as many corporate and instructional videos and commercials. This format evolved during the early days of live television. Here, the page is divided in half, with all the video elements on the left and all the corresponding audio elements on the right. This is useful for directors and crew to see exactly what shot accompanies what line of dialogue or sound cue. Figure 10.3 provides a sample page of a two-column script were *La Llorona* to be written in this format.

As with screenplays, some software programs format the two-column script for you. Also, templates might be available for downloading into word-processing programs. I find it easiest to use the "table" function of Microsoft Word. I insert a two-column table. I then type the video description in ALL CAPS (more below) in the left cell and press the tab key once to jump over to the corresponding cell in the right column for the audio (lowercase for spoken words, ALL CAPS for others, more below). Pressing the tab key again returns to a new cell in the left column, with the next tab going again to the right column. This procedure lines up each video description in a single cell to the left with its corresponding audio in the adjacent single cell to the right. During rewriting, even if I add or delete words, the corresponding cells remain aligned. When I'm done, if I don't want the borders around all the cells, I "select all" and choose "no border" from the border menu.

As with the other formats, there are variations of the two-column format from one studio, network, company, or producer to the next. When you are commissioned to write a script, be sure to use any specific formatting guidelines you are given. That noted, here are the general "rules" for the two-column, split-page, AV script format.

> Margins/Font/Page: same as screenplay—one-inch margins around, 1.5 left allowing for brads rather than staples for longer scripts; Courier New 12-point; page number top right beginning with second page (maybe even followed by a period, as in screenplays).

FADE IN:	
INT. BEDROOM – NIGHT	(MUSIC PLAYS)
A CHILD SLEEPS.	(SFX: MOURNFUL WIND)
AT THE SOUND OF THE WIND,	CHILD: Mama! Mama! [or Papa!
THE CHILD'S EYES OPEN.	Papa!]
	PARENT (O.S.): Yes, my child.
	I'm coming.
PARENT ENTERS.	PARENT (CONT'D): What is it, sweetheart?
	CHILD: The wind, Mama [Papa]. The wind sounds strange, like someone is crying.
	PARENT: Ah, la Llorona.
	CHILD: What is la Llorona?
	PARENT: La Llorona means "the weeping woman." It's an old, old legend.
	CHILD: Tell me, Mama [Papa]. Please tell me so I can sleep.
THE PARENT SETTLES ONTO THE CHILD'S BED.	PARENT: A long time ago, a beautiful woman named Guadalupe lived in a village. She had no husband.

Figure 10.3 Sample first pages of the two-column format, also called the split-page format and the AV format (for audio-visual)

EXT. VILLAGE - DAY OR NIGHT	
VILLAGERS ARE GATHERED AROUND A HUT, MUMBLING.	(MUMBLING OF VILLAGERS)
	(SFX: SCREAMS OF CHILDBIRTH)
	(MUSIC PLAYS)
AN OLD HAG STEPS OUT EXCITEDLY.	OLD HAG: Twins! Guadalupe has given birth to twins. A boy and a girl. But these twins are cursed. They have no Papa.
THE VILLAGERS MUMBLE IN AGREED SHAME AND SHUNNING AND THEN DISPERSE.	(MUMBLING OF VILLAGERS)
	(MUSIC BUILDS TO A FOREBODING CRESCENDO)

[NEW PAGE]

EXT. VILLAGE - DAY	
THE HUT SITS ALONE. THE DOOR OPENS. GUADALUPE EMERGES, CARRYING A BASKET. SHE COMFORTS THE UNSEEN CRYING BABIES.	(MUSIC TRANSITIONS TO DAY)
	(SFX: BIRDS, MORNING SOUNDS)
	(SFX: CRYING BABIES)

Figure 10.3 (continued)

Columns: Video column on the left half of the page, audio column on the right half. Align each shot description, action description, or other visual information in the video column with its corresponding dialogue or sound cue in the audio column. You may label each column at the top, "VIDEO" and "AUDIO," respectively, though the content of each column is obvious so the labels are not really necessary. In the olden days, pages were pre-formatted with the column headings and also a dividing line down the center to make it easy for the script typist to keep things lined up after inserting a page in the typewriter. Using a two-column table in a word-processing program today accomplishes the same alignment.

Capitalization: A recommended convention is to CAPITALIZE every word that is NOT SPOKEN. This includes everything in the video column, as well as character names, music, and sound effects in the audio column. Words for performers to speak are written in regular, "down-style," lowercase letters. This is done because: (a) research shows it is easier for performers to read down-style letters than ALL CAPS, and (b) capitalizing all non-spoken words helps distinguish them from dialogue.

Video: The video column can contain four types of descriptions, depending on the nature of each shot: (1) shot size—LS, MS, CU, etc. (abbreviations for "long shot," "medium shot," and "close-up," respectively); (2) subject of shot—LS BEDROOM, MS CHILD, etc.; (3) action description or blocking notes—PARENT ENTERS ROOM, SITS ON BED, etc.; (4) special visual cues, such as camera movements (e.g., PAN, DOLLY, ZOOM), visual effects (e.g., FLASH OF LIGHT, SMOKE), or transitions (e.g., DISSOLVE, WIPE).

Audio: The audio column may also contain four types of information: (a) character names, (b) dialogue, (c) music, and (d) sound effects—"SFX." In addition to the recommendation that only spoken dialogue be written in regular, lowercase, down-style letters, while everything else be written in ALL CAPS, some writers place music and SFX cues in parentheses and underline them in order to make them REALLY distinguishable from dialogue. This goes back to the days of radio scripts when the convention was to write sound cues in ALL CAPS, (in parentheses), and underlined. Character names may be centered over their respective dialogue, or they may appear on the first line of dialogue, followed by a colon. In the sample *La Llorona* script, the latter option is used because it saves a few lines of space.

Spacing: Two-column scripts may be either single- or double-spaced. Double-spacing is preferred for production scripts because there is more room for changes and notes. Single-spacing is acceptable for non-production uses, such as spec scripts and publication. In any case, double-spacing should be used *between* video descriptions and *between* different characters, even if single-spacing is used *within* a single description or line of dialogue.

Stage-Play Format

While this book targets screenwriters, many of these concepts apply to stage plays. To be sure, there are differences to consider in writing a story that is staged for a camera and edited for later viewing on a screen and a story that is staged live in an auditorium in front of an audience (e.g., Manvell 1979), or perhaps a multi-camera, live-audience format that combines both. Still, dramatic writing for the stage includes developing characters who engage in plots in which they attempt to resolve conflicts, arcing along the way to their final resolutions, with other characters and sometimes secondary and tertiary stories along the way. For this reason, as a bonus to you readers, I provide here an overview of the stage-play format. If *La Llorona* were written for the stage, the first two pages might look something like Figure 10.4.

As with other script formats, there are variations to the basic guidelines. Different companies might require slight differences in

ACT 1

Scene 1

SETTING: A child's bedroom. Night. The bed cover, toys, and stuffed animals suggest a happy, optimistic, and curious child.

AT RISE: The CHILD is asleep in bed. Music plays. The sound of a mournful wind suddenly disturbs the night. The child awakens with a start, sits up, and cries out.

CHILD
Mama! Mama! [or Papa! Papa!]

PARENT
(off)
Yes, my child, I'm coming.
(The PARENT enters.)
What is it, sweetheart?

CHILD
The wind, Mama [Papa]. The wind sounds strange, like someone is crying.

PARENT
Ah, la Llorona.

CHILD
What is la Llorona?

PARENT
La Llorona means "the weeping woman." It's an old, old legend.

CHILD
Tell me, Mama [Papa]. Please tell me so I can sleep.

(The PARENT settles onto the child's bed.)

PARENT
A long time ago, a beautiful woman named Guadalupe lived in a village. She had no husband.

(BLACKOUT)

(END OF SCENE)

Figure 10.4 Sample first pages of the stage-play format

ACT 1

Scene 2

SETTING: Outside a simple hut in a small village long ago. Night. The setting suggests a time of superstition.

AT RISE: VILLAGERS mill around the hut, carrying torches and mumbling. From inside we hear the screams of childbirth. The screams stop. An OLD HAG emerges excitedly. Music plays.

OLD HAG
Twins! Guadalupe has given birth to twins. A boy and a girl. But these twins are cursed. They have no Papa.

(The VILLAGERS mumble in agreed shame and shunning and then disperse. The music builds to a foreboding crescendo. Then the lights, music, and sounds transition to a new day. It is morning. Birds sing. New music plays. A figure emerges from the hut. It is GUADALUPE. She carries a basket, from which comes the sound of crying babies. She begins to walk through the village. The OLD HAG and VILLAGERS reappear, gathering around her, forming a gantlet. They curse and hiss at her. She walks stoically through the crowd to the edge of the village. She stops for a moment. Then she walks off.)

(BLACKOUT)

(END OF SCENE)

Figure 10.4 (*continued*)

formatting unique to that company. Always know the target of your play—who you would like to read it—and follow the guidelines of that target. Here I present the most general "rules," adapted from the Cary Playwrights Forum (caryplaywrightsforum.org<http://www.caryplaywrightsforum.org/>).

There are also some software programs that format the stage play for you, and templates might be available for downloading into word-processing programs. In terms of dialogue and stage directions, the stage-play format appears to be the reverse of the film screenplay format. Dialogue is written margin-to-margin in stage plays, and stage directions and action descriptions are indented—the opposite of the screenplay format. The stage-play format has evolved from the beginning of live entertainment, which is sometimes (but not always) heavier on dialogue than filmed entertainment, so it makes sense that dialogue would be written across the width of the page and action would be indented to stand out from the spoken words. Conversely, the film-script format has evolved only since motion image photography was invented, and with the camera's ability to move anywhere, some (but not all) filmed entertainment is heavier on action than dialogue, so that medium's format has action written across the page width with dialogue indented to set it apart.

In other ways, the stage and screen script formats are similar, such as page margins and type font. Other elements are unique to each, such as the "SETTINGS" and "AT RISE" descriptions at the start of each new act and scene in a stage play. Whatever the format—stage or film or television—all share the rule of thumb that one page of script equals about one minute of time on the stage or screen.

<u>Margins/Font/Page</u>: same as screenplay—one-inch margins around, 1.5 left allowing for brads rather than staples for longer scripts; Courier New 12-point; page number top right.

<u>Acts and scenes</u>: Act designation 4 inches from left edge, ALL CAPS, underlined, followed by a double space and the scene designation, also 4 inches from left, down-style, also underlined.

SETTING: The word "SETTING" double-spaced below act and scene designations, ALL CAPS, left margin, followed by a colon, then the description of the stage setting (e.g., time, place, furniture, atmosphere, etc.), 4 inches from left edge (directly under Act and scene designations).

AT RISE: The words "AT RISE" double-spaced below setting, ALL CAPS, left margin, followed by colon, then the description of the situation and action that is taking place when the curtain rises (e.g., what people are doing, etc.), 4 inches from left (directly under "SETTING").

Character names: double-spaced below previous line, ALL CAPS, 4 inches from left edge (directly under "SETTING" and "AT RISE").

Dialogue: single-spaced below character, lowercase down-style, and the reverse of a film script—goes margin-to-margin rather than indented.

Stage directions: single-spaced below character (either character name or dialogue), lowercase down-style, in parentheses, and the reverse of a film script—indented left and right—specifically 2.75 inches left and 2.5 inches right. Character names are CAPITALIZED in stage directions.

Curtain/Blackout/End: double space below last line, indent 4 inches from left edge (directly under "setting," "at rise," and character names), ALL CAPS, in parentheses, "(BLACKOUT)" or "(CURTAIN), then double space, same style, "(END OF SCENE)" OR "(END OF ACT)."

Summary

Writers should be prepared to write for any medium, including *film*, *television*, *stage*, and *new media*. It is important to know and apply the differences between the script formats for these different storytelling vehicles. Studio, network, and independent executives and producers expect scripts to be in the correct format. (1) A *film* script should look like a film script. (2) A *sitcom* script should be presented as a sitcom script. (3) A *two-column* script should be in two columns. (4) A *stage* play should read like a stage play. This chapter offers an overview of the major guidelines for these four script formats. For additional help in formatting scripts, I recommend searching for any of the excellent books and online resources on this topic.

Reflection and Discussion

1. Consider the scene you created in the previous chapters' "Reflection and Discussion" exercises. If you were to rewrite that scene for the live stage, what changes would you make to take advantage of that medium?
2. Consider a film that was adapted from a stage play. If you are already familiar with both the movie and the play, use that. If not, research the internet (e.g., the Internet Movie Data Base, imdb.com http://www.imdb.com/) to find a film that was adapted from the play, watch it, and also read the stage play (online or visit the library). What differences do you observe between the film and stage versions? Why do you think the film's writers, producers, and director made those changes for the screen?
3. While most successful writers today write for both stage and screen, many prefer one medium over the other. Some prefer the stage because of the intimacy of the live audience. Others prefer television because of the challenge of creating a story every week. Still others prefer film because of the limitless possibilities of changing place and time. Some others prefer the shorter, rapid-fire writing of **webisodes**—internet mini-films—or **mobisodes**— mini-films for mobile devices. Reflect on your own writing style and the types of stories you like to tell. Do you think you prefer one of these media more than the others, or do you feel equally at home writing for them all? Why?

References

Abdullah, Adnan. K. 1985. *Catharsis in literature.* Bloomington: Indiana University Press.

Alten, Stanley R. 2005. *Audio in media,* 7th ed. Belmont, CA: Wadsworth.

Aristotle. c. 335 BCE. *Poetics*, translated by G. F. Else. Ann Arbor: University of Michigan Press, 1970.

Armer, Alan A. 1989. *Directing television and film*, 2nd ed. Belmont, CA: Wadsworth.

— 1993. *Writing the screenplay: TV and film*, 2nd ed. Belmont, CA: Wadsworth.

Bailey, Anne Howard. 1957. "Notes on 'the narrow man.'" In *Television plays for writers,* edited by Abraham Saul Burack. Boston: The Writer.

Balazs, Bela. 1953. *Theory of the film: Character and growth of a new art.* New York: Roy.

Bazin, André. 1967. *What is cinema?* Vol. 1, translated by Hugh Gray. Berkeley: University of California Press.

Berger, Arthur Asa. 1999. *An anatomy of humor.* Piscataway, NJ: Transaction.

Berlyne, Daniel E. 1972. "Humor and its kin." In *The psychology of humor,* edited by Jeffrey H. Goldstein and Paul E. McGhee, 43–60. New York: Academic Press.

Bordwell, David, and Kristin Thompson. 2010. *Film art: An introduction*, 9th ed. New York: McGraw-Hill.

Boggs, Joseph, and Dennis Petrie. 2011. *The art of watching films*, 8th ed. New York: McGraw-Hill, 2004.

Brecht, Bertolt. 1927. "Problems of the epic theatre." In *Brecht on theatre: The development of an aesthetic*, 1st ed., edited and translated by John Willett. New York: Hill & Wang, 1994.

Buddhist Studies, Unit Six: The four immeasurables. 2008. Buddha Dharma Education Association and BuddhaNet. Accessed January 15, 2013. http://www.buddhanet.net/e-learning/buddhism/bs-s15.htm

Burdick, Jacques. 1974. *Theater.* New York: Newsweek Books.

Campbell, Joseph. 1949. *The hero with a thousand faces*, 3rd ed. Novato, CA: New World Library, 2008.

Cary Playwrights Forum. 2013. Accessed February 4, 2013. http://www.caryplaywrightsforum.org/wp-content/uploads/2012/07/CPF_play_formatting2.pdf

Charney, Maurice. 2005. *Comedy high and low: Introduction to the experience of comedy*, 2nd ed. New York: Peter Lang.

Compesi, Ronald J. 2006. *Video field production and editing*, 7th ed. Boston: Allyn & Bacon, an imprint of Pearson.

Cook, David A. 2008. *A history of narrative film*, 4th ed. New York: W.W. Norton.

Cooper, Lane. 1923. *The poetics of Aristotle: Its meaning and influence.* Ithaca, NY: Cornell University Press.

Dyas, Ronald D. 1993. *Screenwriting for television and film.* Madison, WI: Brown & Benchmark.

Desberg, Peter, and Jeffrey Davis. 2010. *Show me the funny: At the writers' table with Hollywood's top comedy writers.* New York: Sterling.

Edson, Eric. 2011. *The story solution: 23 actions all great heroes must take.* Studio City, CA: Michael Wiese Productions.

Egri, Lajos. 1946. *The art of dramatic writing*. New York: Merricat Publications, 2009.
Eisenstein, Sergei M. 1942. *The film sense*. Edited and translated by Jay Leyda. New York: Harcourt Brace.
— 1949. *Film form: Essays in film theory*. Edited and translated by Jay Leyda. New York: Harcourt Brace, 1949.

Feinberg, Leonard. 1978. *The secret of humor*. New York: Rodopi.
Field, Syd. 2005. *Screenplay: The foundations of screenwriting*, rev. ed. New York: Delta.
Fink, Edward J. 2013 Spring/Summer. "Writing *The Simpsons*: A case study of comic theory." *Journal of film and video* 65.1–2:43–55.
Foust, James C., Edward J. Fink, and Lynne S. Gross. 2012. *Video production: Disciplines and techniques*. Scottsdale, AZ: Holcomb Hathaway.
Freud, Sigmund. 1905. *The joke and its relation to the unconscious*. New York: Norton, 2003.
— 1917. *A general introduction to psychoanalysis*. New York: Washington Square Press, 1952.
— 1922. *Beyond the pleasure principle*. Whitefish: Kessinger, 2010.
— 1923. *The ego and the id*. London: Hogarth Press, 1949.

Gassner, John. 1966. "Catharsis and the modern theatre." In *The idea of tragedy*, edited by Carl Frederick Benson and T. Littleton. Glenview, IL: Scott, Foresman & Co.
Gorbman, Claudia. 1987. *Unheard melodies: Narrative film music*. Bloomington: Indiana University Press.
Gross, Lynne S. 2009. *Digital moviemaking*, 7th ed. Belmont, CA: Wadsworth.
Grotjahn, Martin. 1966. *Beyond laughter: Humor and the subconscious*. New York: McGraw-Hill.
Gruner, Charles. R. 1999. *The game of humor: A comprehensive theory of why we laugh*. Piscataway, NJ: Transaction.

Hatlen, Theodore W. 1991. *Orientation to the theatre*, 5th ed. Boston: Pearson.

Herman, Lewis. 1974. *A practical manual of screen playwriting for theatre and television films*. New York: New American Library.

Hilliard, Robert L. 2012. *Writing for television, radio, and new media*, 10th ed. Belmont, CA: Wadsworth.

Hodge, Francis. 1999. *Play irecting: Analysis, communication and style*, 5th ed. Englewood Cliffs, NJ: Prentice Hall.

Hunter, Lew. 2004. *Lew Hunter's screenwriting 434*, rev. ed. New York: Perigree Trade.

Hyde, Stuart. 2003. *Idea to script: Storytelling for today's media*. Boston: Allyn & Bacon, an imprint of Pearson.

Jung, Carl. 1921. *Psychological types*. Princeton: Princeton University Press, 1971.

Katz, Steven D. 1991. *Film directing, shot by shot: Visualizing from concept to screen*. Studio City, CA: Michael Wiese Productions.

—— 1992. *Film directing, cinematic motion: A workshop for staging scenes*. Studio City, CA: Michael Wiese Productions.

Keough, William. 1998. "The violence of American humor." In *What's so funny? Humor in American culture*, edited by Nancy A. Walker. Wilmington: Scholarly Resources, 133–43.

Kitatani, Kenji. 1985. *Television production theory and aesthetic analysis*. Bloomington: Indiana University (unpublished).

Lee, Lance. 2001. *A poetics for screenwriters*. Austin: University of Texas Press.

London, Kurt. 1936. *Film music*. London: Faber & Faber.

Lucey, Paul. 1996. *Story sense: Writing story and script for feature films and television*. New York: McGraw-Hill.

MacHovec, Frank J. 2012. *Humor: History, theory, applications*. Bloomington, IN: iUniverse.

Mamer, Bruce. 2008. *Film production technique: Creating the accomplished image*, 5th ed. Belmont, CA: Wadsworth

Manvell, Roger. 1979. *Theater and film: A comparative study of the two forms of dramatic art and of the problems of adaptation of stage plays into films.* Cranbury, NJ: Associated University Press.

McKee, Robert. *Story: Substance, structure, style, and the principles of screenwriting.* Regan Books, 2010.

Medoff, Norman J., and Edward J. Fink. 2012. *Portable video: News and field production*, 6th ed. Boston: Focal Press.

Meyer, John C. 2000. "Humor as a double-edged sword: Four functions of humor in communication." *Communication theory* 10.3:310–31.

Miller, William Charles. 1997. *Screenwriting for film and television.* Boston: Pearson.

Millerson, Gerald. 2012. *Television production*, 15th ed. Boston: Focal Press.

Morley, John. 2008. *Scriptwriting for high-impact videos*, 2nd ed. Bloomington, IN: iUniverse.

Morreall, John. 2009. *Comic relief: A comprehensive philosophy of humor.* Hoboken: Wiley-Blackwell.

Musburger, Robert B. 2010. *Single-camera video production*, 5th ed. Boston: Focal Press.

Muller, Robert, ed. 1973. *The television dramatist.* London: Paul Eleck.

Myers & Briggs Foundation. 2013. Accessed January 24. http://myersbriggs.org/

Nettleton, George H., Arthur E. Case, and George Winchester Stone Jr., eds. 1975. *British dramatists from Dryden to Sheridan*, 2nd ed. Carbondale: Southern Illinois University Press.

Nicoll, Allardyce. 1931. *The theory of drama.* London: George G. Harrop,
— 1936. *Film and theatre.* New York: Thomas Y. Crowell.

O'Bannon, Dan, with Matt R. Lohr. 2012. *Dan O'Bannon's guide to screenplay structure.* Studio City, CA: Michael Wiese Productions.

Owens, Jim, and Gerald Millerson. 2011. *Video production handbook*, 5th ed. Boston: Focal Press.

Parker, W. Oren, R. Craig Wolf, and Dick Block. 2008. *Scene design and stage lighting*, 9th ed. Belmont, CA: Wadsworth.

Phillips, William H. 2009. *Film: An introduction*, 4th ed. New York: Bedford St. Martin's.

Portmann, John. 2000. *When bad things happen to other people*. New York: Routledge.

Rapp, Albert. 1951. *The origins of wit and humor*. New York: Dutton.

Raskin, Victor. 1984. *Semantic mechanisms of humor*. New York: Springer.

Richards, Ron. 1992. *A Director's Method for Film and Television*. Boston: Focal Press.

Rilla, Wolf Peter. 1973. *The writer and the screen: On writing for film and television*. London: Witt Allen.

Riso, Don Richard, and Russ Hudson. 1996. *Personality types: Using the Enneagram for self-discovery*, rev ed. New York: Houghton Mifflin.

Rosenthal, J. 1973. "Essay on 'Another Sunday' and 'Sweet F.A. 93.'" In *The television dramatist*, edited by Robert Muller. London: Paul Eleck.

Roth, Lane. 1983. *Film semiotics, Metz, and Leone's trilogy*. New York: Garland Press.

Salvaggio, Jerry Lee. 1980. *A theory of film language*. New York: Arno Press.

Schaeffer, Neill. 1981. *The art of laughter*, New York: Columbia University Press.

Selbo, Jule. 2007. *Gardner's guide to screenplay: From idea to successful script*. Washington, DC: Garth Gardner.

—— 2008. *Gardner's guide to screenplay: The rewrite*. Washington, DC: Garth Gardner.

Seger, Linda. 2010. *Making a good script great*, 3rd ed. Los Angeles: Silman-James Press.

Sharrer, Erica, Andrea Bergstrom, Angela Paradise, and Qianqing Ren. 2006. "Laughing to keep from crying: Humor and aggression in television commercial content." *Journal of broadcasting & electronic media* 50.4:615–34.

Shurcliff, Arthur. 1968. "Judged humor, arousal, and the relief theory." *Journal of personality and social psychology* 8.4:360–63.

Skiles, Marlin. 1976. *Music scoring for TV and motion pictures.* Blue Ridge Summit, PA: Tab Books.

Smiley, Sam. 2006. *Playwriting: The structure of action*, 2nd ed. New Haven, CT: Yale University Press.

Stanislavski, Constantin. 1936. *An actor prepares.* Translated by Elizabeth Reynolds Hapgood, New York: Theatre Arts.

Stempel, Tom. 1982. *Screenwriting.* San Diego: A.S. Barnes.

Timm, Larry M. 2003. *The soul of cinema: An appreciation of film music*, rev. ed. Upper Saddle River, NJ: Prentice Hall.

Vogler, Chris. 2007. *The writer's journey: Mythic structure for writers*, 3rd ed. Studio City, CA: Michael Wiese Productions.

Walters, Roger L. 1994. *Broadcast writing: Principles and practices*, 2nd ed. New York: McGraw-Hill.

Watson, Walter. 2012. *The lost second book of Aristotle's "Poetics."* Chicago: University of Chicago Press.

Wexman, Virginia W. 2009. *A history of film*, 7th ed. Boston: Allyn & Bacon, an imprint of Pearson.

Willis, Edgar E., and Camille D'Arienzo. 1993. *Writing scripts for television, radio, and film*, 3rd ed. Fort Worth, TX: Harcourt Brace Jovanovich.

Winston, Douglas Garrett. 1973. *The screenplay as literature.* Rutherford, NJ: Fairleigh Dickinson University Press.

Withers, Robert S. 1983. *Introduction to film.* New York: Barnes & Noble.

Zettl, Herbert. 2011. *Television production handbook*, 11th ed. Belmont, CA: Wadsworth.

— 2013. *Sight, sound, motion: Applied media aesthetics*, 7th ed. Belmont, CA: Wadsworth.

Zillmann, Dolph. 1971. "Excitation transfer in communication-mediated aggressive behavior." *Journal of experimental social psychology* 7:419–34.

Ziv, Avner. 1984. *Personality and sense of humor.* New York: Springer.

Index

10 Things I Hate about You 79

Abbott and Costello 156
abstract 121
absurd 160
Achilles' heel 48
Act 1 16–19
Act 15
Act 2A 19–23
Act 2B 23–26
Act 3 26–29
act breaks 40, 176
action 29, 162
action line 180, 183
ADR *see* automated dialogue replacement 112
Aeschylus 87
Aesop 81, 82
Aliens 158
Amadeus 80, 107, 110, 126
Amazing Spider-Man, The 17
An Affair to Remember 45
Angels & Demons 119
angle 182
angle on 129
Annie Hall 159

antagonist 13, 51–55
arc 22, 49
Aristophanes 152
Aristotle 2, 3, 11, 44, 73, 84, 106, 116, 141, 143
A-story 15
at rise 194
audience 142
aural gags 155
automated (automatic) dialogue replacement 112
Avatar 126
AV format (audio-visual format) 183

back lot 119
back story 30, 59
Batman 52, 53, 54
beat 30, 58, 181
Being John Malkovich 93
Big Bang Theory 182
biopic 107
Black Maria 122
Blazing Saddles 96, 109, 170
blocking 129
Bonanza 148
bookend 17

boom shot 130
brad 177
Brecht, Bertolt 62
B–story 15
Butch Cassidy and the Sundance Kid 46

Cabinet of Dr. Caligari, The 132
Cameron, James 126
Campbell, Joseph 36
Capote 107
Cary Playwrights Forum 193
Casablanca 20, 22, 100–101
catharsis 142, 164; emotional excitation 143; emotive arousal 143; intellectual understanding 143; cognition 143
Celtx 175
CGI *see* computer-generated imagery
CGI-enhanced 120
Chaplin, Charlie 158, 159
character 44, 142
character deficit 48
character line 181, 183, 191
Chavez 107
Chinatown 90
choleric 65
Christmas Carol, A 132
Churchill, Winston 170
cinéma vérité 123
Citizen Kane 31, 166
cliffhanger 29
climax 16, 27
close on 182
close-up 14, 129, 189
Coen, Joel and Ethan 91, 165
comedy 2, 28, 146 151; success 146
comedy of manners 152

comic relief 147
comic structure 166
commedia dell'arte 152
commissioned script 176
complications 30
comprehensibility 96
computer-generated imagery 120, 131
confidant 56
conflict 1
costume 123
costume drama 124
counterpoint music 110
coverage 15
crane shot 130
Crash 57, 139
C-story 15
CU *see* close-up
curtain/blackout/end 194
cut 131
Cyrano de Bergerac 152, 154

Dallas 149
Dances with Wolves 17
dark comedy 165
Da Vinci Code, The 119
Day–Lewis, Daniel 63
Death of a Salesman 16, 69
denouement 28
description line 180
deus ex machina 42
development 176
dialectic conflict 110
dialogue 29, 84, 162
dialogue line 181, 183, 191
dianoia 73
Dickson, William 122
Die Hard 47

Index

diegetic music 108
direct address 130
Dirty Harry 100
dissolve 131, 181
Dr. Strangelove 134
Doctor Zhivago 140
documentary 107
dolly shot 129
Don Giovanni 107
double entendre 170
double whammy 168
Downton Abbey 70
Dracula 123
drama 1
Drew's Script-O-Rama 175
dual meaning 102
Dumb & Dumber 155

Eastwood, Clint 59
economy of writing 85
Edison, Thomas 122
editing 131
Edson, Eric 37–39
Egri, Lajos 68
Eisenstein, Sergei 110
Elf 158
empathy 59
enlightenment 143
Enneagram 65–66
ensemble 45
epic theater 62
epicism *see* epic theater
Equus 80
Erin Brockovich 125
E.T. 99
Ethos 44, 59, 142
Euripides 87
exaggeration 161

Excitation Transfer Theory 159
exposition 30
Expressionism 123
EXT. *see* exterior
exterior 120, 180
extraordinary person in ordinary situation 47

fade in 180
fade out 181
farce 160
Fargo 165
Field of Dreams 102
Field, Syd 34
final cut 12
Final Draft 175
Finding Nemo 12, 26, 27, 28, 48, 51, 53, 54, 56, 95
first person 130
fish out of water 158
flashback 31
fly page 176
Foley artist 111
foreshadow 23
Forrest Gump 17, 48, 57, 148
fours humors 64–65
fourth wall 130, 159
framing structure 17
Frasier 48, 156
Freud, Sigmund 66, 67, 164
functionaries 57–58

Galen 64
gallows humor 165
Gangs of New York 63
Gladiator 20, 27, 28, 51, 157
Glass Menagerie, The 140
Godfather, The 70, 101

Index

Godfather: Part II, The 137
Gone with the Wind 49, 78, 100, 130
Good Morning, Vietnam 114

hair 125
Hamlet 69, 97, 98, 136, 156
Hangover, The 45
happy ending 157
heightened realism 91
high comedy 152, 156, 162
high-key lighting 121
Hippocrates 64
Hobbit, The 12, 127
Home Alone 77, 171
Homeland 149
How the Grinch Stole Christmas 127
human v. environment 53
human v. human 52
human v. self 54
Hunter, Lew 34
hybris (also hubris) 61

illogical situations 160
I Love Lucy 155
I'm No Angel 99
Importance of Being Earnest, The 152, 162, 163
Impressionism 123
inciting incident 18
Incongruity Theory 157
innuendo 167, 169
insert 182
INT. see interior
intended meaning 102
interior 120, 180
Iron Lady, The 127

Jackson, Peter 127
James Bond 51
Jaws 18, 100
Jerry Maguire 45, 100
Julie & Julia 127
Jung, Carl 66–67
Jurassic Park 16, 18, 134

Keaton, Buster 130
key 131
King Kong 130
Kiss Me Kate 79
Kung Fu Panda 23

La Llorona 4–10, 17, 19, 20, 22, 23, 25, 26, 27, 29, 48, 51, 54, 59, 60, 61, 73, 74, 75, 96, 107, 110, 112, 113, 117, 118, 136, 137, 139, 143, 145, 146, 147, 176, 177, 178–79, 184–85, 187–88, 191–92
Last of the Mohicans, The 63
laughter 143
legend 142
leitmotif 109, 141
Les Misérables 125
lesson 74
lexis 84
lighting 121
Lincoln 12, 51, 63, 127
Lion King, The 98–99
literal meaning 102
location 119
logical extreme 160
log line 177
long shot 14, 129, 189
looping see automated dialogue replacement 112

Lord of the Rings, The 127
Lost 149
low comedy 152, 156, 164
lower-third 131
low-key lighting 121
LS *see* long shot
Lucas, George 26
Lysistrata 164

M*A*S*H 143
MacGuffin 69
McKee, Robert 25
Mad About You 137
main plot *see* A-story
makeup 125
Maltese Falcon, The 127
Mamet, David 89
mask 128
master scene 176
master shot 15
medium shot 14, 129, 189
melancholic 64
Méliès, George, 130
melodrama 28, 148
melos 106
Memento 32, 33
mentor 56
metadiegetic music 109
metaphor 139; affective manipulation 139; cognitive manipulation 139;
Midnight Express 158
midpoint 22
midpoint crisis 16
midpoint ordeal 21
mise-en-scène 132
Mission Impossible 93
mobisode 12, 195

Modern Family 169, 183
Modern Times 134
Monster's Ball 127
montage 24, 131, 182
Monty Python and the Holy Grail 70, 171
Monty Python's Flying Circus 160, 170
Mother Courage 62
Movie Magic 175
MS *see* medium shot
mudita 157
music 106, 107–111
My Big Fat Greek Wedding 168
Myers-Briggs 67
My Left Foot 63
myth 142
mythos 11

narrative 107
naturalism 88, 120, 144
Network 100
no lasting harm 146, 157, 165
nondiegetic music 109
Nonrealism 145
nonrealistic set 120
no real harm *see* no lasting harm
Nosferatu 123
Notting Hill 157

O.S. *see* off-screen
obsession 69
Oedipus Rex, Oedipus the King 27, 62, 86, 137, 146, 151, 157
off-screen 181
One Flew Over the Cuckoo's Nest 69
one-liners 170

opsis 116
ordinary person in extraordinary situation 47
Othello 146
outline 174
overwriting 85, 107, 117, 131

panning shot 130
Pan's Labyrinth 134
parallel music 109
parenthtetical 181
passion 69
pathos 60, 142, 143
payoff 29, 166, 167
PDF *see* Portable Document Format
pedestal shot 130
peeling the onion 31, 59
phlegmatic 64
physical features 127
physical set 120
physiology 68
Pink Panther 166
Pirates of the Caribbean: Dead Man's Chest 126
pitch meeting 176
Plautus 152
Player, The 15
plot 11, 141
plot point 21
plot point one 19
plot point two 25
Poeticism 86
Poetics 2, 114, 151
point of attack 16
point of view 74, 130, 182
Polar Express, The 70
Portable Document Format 175

POV *see* point of view
Pretty Woman 157
production script 176
properties 127
props *see* properties
protagonist 12, 44–51
Psycho 110, 159
Psychoanalytic Theory 164
psychology 68
Pulp Fiction 32, 33, 88
Punch and Judy 155
punch line 167
put-downs 170

Raiders of the Lost Ark 70, 166
Rain Man 1988
Raising Arizona 58, 91
raisonneur 57
realism 89, 144
realistic set 120
Relief Theory *see* Psychoanalytic Theory
reportorial shot 130
resolution 16
Return of Martin Guerre, The 110
rewriting 86, 176
rising action 21
Rob Roy 113
Romanticism 144
Romeo and Juliet 70, 157
Rostand, Edmund 151, 154
Rule of Threes 156, 167
running gag 164, 168

satire 160
sanguine 64
Sausalito 123
Saving Private Ryan 132

Scary Movie 159
scene 15
Schadenfreude 148, 156, 165
Schindler's List 52, 53, 54, 100, 146
screenplay format 176
second person 130
Seger, Linda 34
Seinfeld 70, 80
Selbo, Jule 34–35
self-reflexivity 159
sequence 15
sequence shot 15
set 119
setting 194
setup 15, 166, 167
shadow 121
Shaffer, Peter 80
Shakespeare 97
She Done Him Wrong 169, 170
Shining, The 123
shot 14
Shrek 74
sight gags 151, 155
Simply Scripts 175
Simpsons, The 164, 168
sitcom format 182
Skyfall 12
slapstick 154
slug line 120, 180, 183
smash cut 132
sociology 68
Sophocles 87
sound 106
sound effects 111
Sound of Music, The 32
sound stage 119
South Pacific 74
spaghetti western 59

spark 26
spec script 104, 176
special effects makeup 126
special visual effects 130
spectacle 116
Speed 3
Spielberg, Steven, 52
Split-page format 183
staff writer 86
stage directions 194
stage play format 190
stakes 25
Star Wars 20, 22, 23, 26, 49, 56, 113, 127, 141
Star Trek 118
stereotypes 161
story-within-a-story 17
studio 119
style 144
subclimax 19
subplot 13; *see also* B-story and C-story
subtext 30, 102
superimposition 131
Superiority Theory 162
Superman 47, 48
supporting characters 55–57
Surrealism 123
suspense 29
suspension of disbelief 159
symbol 140
Symbolism 121
sympathy 59
synergy 4
synopsis 74, 177

talent 127
Taming of the Shrew, The 79, 138

Tarantino, Quentin 88
Tension 21
Thelma and Louise 46, 47, 56
theme 73, 142
There Will Be Blood 63
third person 130
Three Stooges, The 155
three-act structure 11–14
three-dimensional characters 68
Threepenny Opera, The 62
three-point lighting 123
timbre 112
Titanic 58, 131
To Kill a Mockingbird 50
Tortoise and the Hare, The 81
Touch of Evil 15
Toy Story 127
tracking shot 129
tragedy 2, 27, 146; ruin 146
tragicomedy 149
treatment 174
Trip to the Moon, A 130
turnaround 19
two-column script format 183

unexpected surprise 158
unity 135
unity of action 135
unity of theme 137
unity of time and place 136
universality 141
unmasking 58

Untouchables, The 89
Up 16, 25, 26, 27, 28, 85, 93, 94

V.O. *see* voice-over
Vertigo 48
virtual set 120
Vogler, Chris 35–37
voice 112
voice-over 181

Waiting for Godot 33, 104, 149
Waking Ned Devine 20, 21
walkie-talkie 107
wardrobe 123
webisode 12, 195
West Side Story 157
What a Wonderful World 114
Wicked 79
wide shot 15, 129
Wilde, Oscar 163
Will & Grace 113
Williams, Tennessee 141
Winnie the Pooh and the Blustery Day 123
wipe 131, 181
Witness 18, 19, 20, 22, 23, 25, 26, 27, 28
Wiz, The 79
Wizard of Oz, The 30, 48, 50, 58, 69, 75, 94, 123, 131

Zero Dark Thirty 118
zoom-in 129
zoom-out 129

Taylor & Francis
eBooks
FOR LIBRARIES

ORDER YOUR FREE 30 DAY INSTITUTIONAL TRIAL TODAY!

Over 22,000 eBook titles in the Humanities, Social Sciences, STM and Law from some of the world's leading imprints.

Choose from a range of subject packages or create your own!

Benefits for you
- Free MARC records
- COUNTER-compliant usage statistics
- Flexible purchase and pricing options

Benefits for your user
- Off-site, anytime access via Athens or referring URL
- Print or copy pages or chapters
- Full content search
- Bookmark, highlight and annotate text
- Access to thousands of pages of quality research at the click of a button

For more information, pricing enquiries or to order a free trial, contact your local online sales team.

UK and Rest of World: online.sales@tandf.co.uk
US, Canada and Latin America: e-reference@taylorandfrancis.com

www.ebooksubscriptions.com

A flexible and dynamic resource for teaching, learning and research.